LITERARY FORGERIES

LITERARY FORGERIES

BY

J. A. FARRER

WITH AN INTRODUCTION BY ANDREW LANG

LONGMANS, GREEN, AND CO.
39 PATERNOSTER ROW, LONDON
NEW YORK, BOMBAY, AND CALCUTTA
1907
REPUBLISHED BY GALE RESEARCH COMPANY, BOOK TOWER, DETROIT, 1969

Library of Congress Catalog Card Number 68–23156

PREFACE.

THE following chapters are an excursion into those shadier paths of literature where the forger or imitator has for his own ends played on the innocent credulity of mankind. Forbidden paths they may be to the straighter sect of the lovers of literature ; but, having found some delectation in them myself, I have relied on the similar mental constitution of most men for the hope and belief that they may have attractions also for others.

The endeavour has been to present a comprehensive or bird's-eye view of literary forgery, and to convey some idea of the large place it occupies in the intellectual history of our race, and of the considerable influence it has had on the destinies and fortunes of the world. To this end both selection and condensation have been necessary. Where, in so rank an undergrowth, it would be impossible to deal with every tare in the garden of letters, it has seemed best to select for study only the more typical specimens of their kind ; those, that is, which are marked by most literary distinction ; which have presented the most difficult problems; or which have had the most far-reaching influence on the course of human affairs. Round all the specimens so selected a large and extensive literature has grown, and it has been necessary to condense into single chapters the stories of famous controversies, the literature of which often runs into libraries, or is only recoverable from scattered and inaccessible sources.

In these controversies the combatants have often been so equally matched, and both the thrust and the parry been so deftly dealt, that it has frequently been difficult for the mere spectator to adjudge to either side a decisive victory. For this reason finality of judgment is not necessarily involved in the conclusion of a controversy, and many a seemingly settled dispute has in it the germs of renewed activity. The sanctity that the French attach to the *chose jugée* does not appertain to every past decision in the matter of forgery, nor have I deemed it any part of my task simply to register the received opinion. Rather it has seemed better in some cases either to challenge the received opinion or to suggest the exercise of a suspended judgment. Suspense of judgment is one of the highest and most difficult of the intellectual virtues, having many affinities with charity in the moral sphere, and it is because the study of forgery calls so frequently for the exercise of this quality that it affords so excellent a discipline for the faculties of the mind. Nowhere else is required a nicer balancing of opposed arguments; greater need of accuracy of fact; or a more cautious arrival at conclusions.

For the idea of such a survey as I have attempted I am indebted to the chapter on "Literary Forgeries" in D'Israeli's *Curiosities of Literature;* for aid in its execution I am greatly indebted to my friend Mr. Andrew Lang, who has been kind enough to cast a critical and corrective eye over the pages of the proofs. From errors not a few has his skill as a literary detective preserved me, and for those which may remain I claim the sole responsibility. I have also specially to thank him for that portion of the chapter on Ballad-forgers which relates to the interesting ballad of "Auld Maitland," as well as for the concluding paragraph of that chapter. Mr. Lang is so great an authority on ballad-lore that, if I have any regret, it is only that I have not more on that subject to offer from his pen. But the subject is a larger one than can be fairly condensed properly within the compass of one chapter among sixteen; and it must suffice to do little more than indicate how much in this direction still remains to be explored.

As regards the arrangement, although it is most natural to proceed from the more ancient to the more modern, and although this principle has been adopted in the main, yet it has not seemed desirable to adhere too slavishly to the chronological order. Since each chapter treats of a subject distinct in itself, each can be read independently of the rest, and altogether regardless of the order of time.

SUMMARY OF CONTENTS.

CHAPTER IX.

CHAPTER X.

CHAPTER XI.

CHAPTER XII.

CHAPTER XIII.

INTRODUCTION.

THE proverb "let ilka herring hang by its ain heid" is a good one, and Mr. Farrer's book does not need to be accompanied by remarks of mine. In writing a few words preliminary to his book, I accede to his request, while conscious that about his curious topic he knows much more than I do. Literary forgeries are not exhaustively treated in his volume : several volumes would be required by the theme. We might begin with the Homeric poems, of which by far the greater part, if we accept a prevalent theory, is a sort of literary forgery, though done, as a rule, without intent to deceive. Still, it comes to open forgery, when the supposed editor, subsidised by Pisistratus, about B.C. 540, introduces, according to the hypothesis, the speeches of Nestor, for the purpose of glorifying a descendant of Nestor, the tyrant of Athens. On this theory Pisistratus must have been easily pleased, for his ancestor is made a kind of prosing old Dugald Dalgetty, unconsciously humorous.

Indeed, if we believe Greek literary tradition, literary forgery was common as soon as the art of

writing was used for literary purposes. Solon forged
and put "faked" verses into the *Iliad* for political
ends. Onomacritus forged oracles, as the prophecies
of Thomas the Rymer were forged. Are the pre-
dictions of Merlin more authentic, and when, where,
and by whom were they executed?

A base gold coin, a sample of early "smashing,"
has been found in a Scottish Lake Dwelling of about
A.D. 600, proving that Lauder, with his Miltonic
forgeries, was only walking in ancestral paths of
guilt. I daresay that palæolithic forgers falsely
used the mark of some hand then distinguished, the
Landseer of these early sporting sketches, for man
seems from the beginning to have practised every
form of guile. Doubtless rhapsodists in the Ionian
cities listened to some reciter till they knew his lay
by heart and then gave it forth as their own composition : though perhaps that is a case of plagiarism
rather than of forgery.

The entire work of Dares Phrygius, his tale of
Troy, must be a forgery, and it thoroughly took in
the public and the learned of the Middle Ages, who
believed that Dares describes the Trojan war "as
he that saw it".

Perhaps the real author of the *History of the
Trojan War* attributed to Dares was merely a
historical novelist, who, by the usual convention,
pretended to have found an ancient manuscript. In

any case the pseudo Dares told a good tale, and provided Boccaccio, Chaucer, Caxton, Henryson, and Shakespeare with materials for the story of *Troilus and Cressida*.

Perhaps the historical novelist may go too far, despite his privileges. In writing *The Monk of Fife*, years ago, I professed to have discovered the continuation, in French, of a genuine manuscript account of Jeanne d'Arc, begun in Latin by her friend, a Scot, and mysteriously broken off in the middle of a sentence. I even went so far as to forge extracts, in Old French, from the chapel register of St. Catherine of Fierbois, confirmatory of my narrative. Perhaps this was wrong. It was a blunder, if not a crime, for a learned mediævalist could not make out whether he had a modern novel or a fifteenth century document in his hands, while the novel-reading public exclaimed, "Oh, this is a horrid real history!"

Let this be a warning to historical novelists. As to poets, if the public will not read their poems, is it likely that they will be read when expressed in Wardour Street English, Wardour Street spelling, and attributed to a monk of the fourteenth century? Chatterton was guilty of a blunder as well as a crime, with his old Rowley the monk.

Mr. Farrer does not go deep into historical forgeries, like those of Hardynge, intended to prove, by false documents, that Scotland was a dependency

b

of the English Crown. There must be plenty of this kind of forgery. A memorandum in *Foedera*, of 29th September, 1278, concerning the homage paid by Alexander III. of Scotland to Edward I. is proved to be a forgery by means of dates. These show that Alexander, on 16th October, offered his homage, not for Scotland but for lands in England, and that Edward deferred the ceremony. The memorandum about 29th September must have been inserted later, fraudulently and incautiously.

Whether part of the famous casket Letter, No. II., ascribed to Queen Mary, is forged or not, I am unable to decide. It has all the air of being copied from a different document, not by Mary, but by Thomas Crawford, a retainer of Darnley. It is certain, however, that when Mary was a prisoner of Elizabeth, Wharton, an English official in the north, suggested to his Government that letters of the Queen of Scots should be forged and circulated, to her disadvantage. Certainly all parties were unscrupulous about forgery, and I fear that Mary of Guise was involved in the forgery of a letter of the Duke of Chatelherault to the King of France. The Parnell forgeries may not yet be forgotten; they were poorly executed and should not have taken in *The Times*.

We are not quite so easily beguiled as our ancestors. Psalmanazar, in Mr. Farrer's fifth chapter, would have less success than the egregious Rouge-

mont. It is generally thought that Rougemont deceived the British Association, but as far as I know
they only gave him a hearing. Simple as I sit here, I
could not have accepted Rougemont's absurd descrip-
tions of the life of Australian aborigines. Psalmanazar's story of the sacrifice of 20,000 children
yearly is more hard of belief than even the learned
theory that, in times past, a fresh king was sacrificed
yearly. As to Lauder, his forgeries were clever
enough, and safe enough as long as nobody took the
trouble to verify his references. In the long run,
somebody was sure to do so. I cannot but suspect
that the usual account of Lauder's age is erroneous.
If it is correct his existence is a blank till he was
over fifty, and his forgeries are the work of a man
of seventy. Seventy is a late age for entering on a
career of fraud. One of the forged Scott novels takes
for granted that Sir Walter would introduce into the
Rising of 1745 a Countess whose family name is
MacMaggy. Not even an Englishman could invent
a Gaelic name like MacMaggy : it surpasses the
MacCumnor of Dumas, and must be the invention of
a Frenchman.

Mr. Farrer, in a manner unpopular, but scientific,
leaves some of his mysteries unsolved. The case of
Simonides is the most puzzling of any, and

> The tender-hearted scrolls
> Of pure Simonides

seem to clamour for a fresh examination. We now possess many Greek papyri, certainly authentic, of an early date. These were unknown when Simonides produced his early Greek papyri, and perhaps they may repay inspection.

The probable forgery which puzzles me most is the *Vestiarium Scoticum*, a magnificent volume, purporting to date from about 1570-1580, and giving the tartans of the Lowland as well as of the Highland clans. Now it is most improbable that even Highland clans had regular stereotyped distinctive tartans in the sixteenth century, while of Lowland tartans, as of Scott and Ker, no mortal ever heard, outside of the *Vestiarium*.

The manuscript first comes to notice in 1825. Sir Thomas Dick Lauder wrote concerning it to Sir Walter Scott, who turned a sceptical ear. The owner was the father of these two enigmatic men, the "Sobieski Stuarts," claiming to be the grandsons of Prince Charles Edward, through his lawfully begotten son, their father.

Now both Charles and his wife, Louise of Stolberg, denied that there ever was a child by them begotten. The father of the two pretenders was only known in authoritative records as Lieutenant Thomas Allen, R.N., the second son of Captain, later Admiral, R.N.

The two young men averred that their father

possessed, through Prince Charles, a manuscript sixteenth century copy of the *Vestiarium* on vellum, with domestic notes on the fly leaves, written by Queen Mary's Bishop, Lesley, the historian, Bishop of Ross, about his own health. I have seen letters in the hand of Thomas Allen, referring to this copy on vellum. He signs "Mac Garadh," which he took to be the Gaelic form of the surname " Hay". There seems to have been some connexion, real or supposed, between these Allens and the Earls of Errol, and, in 1822, the eldest Sobieski Stuart signs his volume of poems " Iohn *Hay* Allen ".

How the Errol pretensions were to be reconciled with the Stuart pretensions nobody can explain. However, the letters of the paternal Mac Garadh do certainly seem to testify to his possession of the *Vestiarium* on vellum, and, as far as I can judge, these letters are really in the hand of the old gentleman. Eccentric as his sons were, I do not suspect them of forging their father's letters, or suppose that they had the necessary skill, if they had been wickedly inclined. Yet no witness, to my knowledge, has seen the manuscript on vellum. Meanwhile the brothers had another copy, an eighteenth century copy on paper, acquired from an old Highlander, residing in the Cowgate, a teacher of the broad-sword exercise. This copy is extant, and has been tested, as regards

the quality of the ink, the age of the paper, the nature
of the handwriting, and so far, I am given to under-
stand that no fault can be found in it—yet the contents, as concerns the Lowland tartans, have no known
corroboration in history or in art. Further, I have had
opportunities of studying the works and ways of the
two brothers calling themselves "Sobieski Stuarts,"
and it appears to me quite certain that they could
not have written the sixteenth century Scots of the
Vestiarium Scoticum—the necessary learning was not
within their powers. One of them made a kind of
copy of the MS., with amusing caricatures in red
ink, which I have seen ; this copy, of course, made
no pretensions to antiquity.

Thus, to the best of my memory, the question
of the *Vestiarium* stands, and a more inextricable
puzzle in the way of documents I cannot imagine.
What is this eighteenth century manuscript? What
had any mortal to gain by such a minutely skilled
and elaborate forgery? It did not pretend to be
in any way a proof of the Stuart pretensions of the
brothers, yet its contents have no shadow, to my
knowledge, of historical corroboration. (There is an
account of this mystery in *Old and Rare Scottish
Tartans*, by Mr. D. W. Stewart, 1893. I have not
a copy of the book at hand, but Mr. Stewart I think
was as much perplexed as myself.)

Mr. Farrer kindly refers to such slight assistance

as I was able (in the absence of Professor Child's monumental edition of *English and Scottish Popular Ballads*) to give him in the matter of ballad forgeries. In the text is discussed the authenticity of the ballad of *Auld Maitland*, which, in his great edition of Ballads, Professor Child omitted, as a modern forgery. For the reasons given in the text, I am personally convinced that the Ettrick Shepherd was not the forger, and no other modern artist can be, or has been, suggested as the sinner. The Ballad, like *The Outlaw Murray*, does not appear to have been found outside of Ettrick and Yarrow. I have sometimes felt disposed to believe that both ballads are literary imitations, earlier than the eighteenth century, by members of the families of Lethington and Philiphaugh. The Maitlands, from the days of Tom Maitland who "faked" the pamphlet about the Regent Murray and his supporters, were an accomplished set of men of letters. The revelations about Knox and Murray are the one amusing political squib of the Scottish Reformation. By Knox and his friends the joke was not perceived, and, if Thomas Maitland was not guilty, they suspected Satan himself of the authorship.

Really old ballads, transmitted long through oral recitation, exist in many variants. Reciters, perhaps themselves "makers," have added, altered, omitted, to their taste. Sir Walter Scott was the last of the "makers," and, in editing *The Border Minstrelsy*, he used the privilege of the old reciters : he interpolated and improved upon the versions which reached him through oral tradition, or in copies often imperfect.

We have an Otterburn ballad from a manuscript in the British Museum which Professor Child dates about 1550. It is an English version. It opens in the same form as Herd's version, published in 1776, but differs otherwise greatly, and does not contain the words of the dying Douglas :—

> Take thou the vanguard of the three,
> And bury me at the braken bush,
> That stands upon yon lily lee.

Later, Sir Hugh Montgomery, to whom Douglas spoke, vanquishes Percy, and says :—

> O yield thee to yon braken bush
> That grows upon yon lily lee.

Herd's version, imperfect in a stanza, is not suspected of containing literary interpolations. James Hogg obtained recitations of the ballad partly in "plain prose," and lent Scott his version. Douglas speaks :—

> My wound is deep, I fain would sleep,
> Nae mair I'll fighting see,
> Gae lay me in the bracken bush
> That grows in yonder lily lee.

This, of course, is practically Herd's version, and is under no suspicion, save for the first line, " My

wound is deep, I fain would sleep". That line *may*
be by James Hogg. Scott, in the *Minstrelsy*,
adopts it, but, in place of Hogg's "Nae mair I'll
fighting see," gives Herd's "Take thou the van-
guard of the three," with the rest of Herd's verse.
The verse was a great favourite of Sir Walter's : he
quoted it to Lockhart when lying on what he believed
to be his deathbed. The verse is not Scott's ; save
for the first line it is really traditional. Hogg goes
on :—

> But tell na ane of my brave men
>   That I lie bleeding wan,
> But let the name of Douglas still
>   Be shouted in the van.

This verse in the *Minstrelsy* Scott omits : it is
clearly by Hogg. The Shepherd continues in a far
better strain ; his Douglas goes on :—

> And bury me here on this lee
>   Beneath the blooming brier,
> And never let a mortal ken
>   A kindly Scot lyes here.
>
> He liftet up that noble lord
>   Wi' the saut tear in his e'e,
> And hid him in the bracken bush,
>   On yonder lily lee.

Herd has nothing corresponding to this, for Herd's
version does not contain the execution by Montgomery of Douglas's last command. The memory
of Herd's informant may have failed him, for, on
the principles of early poetry, even of the Homeric

epics, we ought to be told that the orders of Douglas *were* obeyed. Hogg's reciters may have supplied his version. Scott prints, with slight verbal alterations, this part of Hogg's version. He thus omits a verse clearly by Hogg himself ; improves, by aid of Hogg, a verse of Herd's traditional text ; and slightly improves two verses of Hogg's version which may possibly enough be traditional.

In *Kinmont Willie* Scott has been suspected of making the whole ballad. His source is not recorded : he says that "it has been much mangled by reciters," and that "some conjectural emendations were absolutely necessary in order to render it intelligible". Apparently his MSS. yield no trace of the ballad as received from reciters. That there really was a ballad appears, I think, from reminiscences of it to be found in Scott of Satchells' rhyming *History* (1638). Certainly, too, Sir Walter never composed *this* stanza :—

> He has called him forty marchmen bauld,
>   I trow they were of his ain name,
> Except Sir Gilbert Elliot, called
>   The Laird of Stobs, *I mean the same.*

Again :—

> 'Twas wind and weet and snaw and sleet

is a regular ballad formula, occurring in Herd's *Sir Patrick Spence*. If Scott, as Professor Child suspects, wrote verse 31, then he took the idea from Satchells, whereas Satchells more probably took it from the ballad. But we may suspect Scott's hand in the ringing stanzas 9-12, on his chief, Buccleuch.

In short, when editing *The Border Minstrelsy*, Scott did not, in the scientific manner, give his versions with textual accuracy, but, as a minstrel himself, used the privilege of all previous reciters. That he actually perverted the Elliot into the Scott version of *Jamie Telfer*, I do not believe, but he imparted poetic merit to his text. Opposite

> The Dinlay snaw was ne'er mair white
> Than the lyart locks o' Harden's hair,

I wrote, long ago, *Aut Jacobus Hogg aut Diabolus*. But certainly it was not Hogg who wrote these lines : it was Sir Walter. The original balladist must have lived, to use a Hibernianism, long after the events recorded in *Jamie Telfer*—for these events never occurred. What did occur, and lent a basis to the ballad, we learn from the despatches of the English officials on the Border in 1596.

I missed my chance as a ballad forger. I was working at MSS. in Abbotsford, when the ballad MSS. were being copied for Professor Child. By engaging an expert I might have had *The Young Ruthven* and *Simmy o' Whythaugh* (*mea carmina*) copied in an old hand on old paper, and thrust into the mass. Then we should have seen whether or not Professor Child could be taken in by a modern ballad forgery.

Recipe to forge a Border Ballad.

Take *The Border Papers*, edited by Joseph Bain
(1890). Select a good rousing incident, say the
slaying of Ridley, at the Newcastle football match
(May, 1599). Write it with as many rhymes in *e*
as possible. Avoid profusion of obsolete words.
Carefully abstain from dropping into poetry. Add
a few anachronisms, and distort historical facts to
taste; employ regular ballad formulæ sparingly and
with caution, strain off, dish, and serve up with
historical notes, adding to taste fables about your
source *à la* Surtees. Remember that nothing can
be less like an old ballad than the ballads of Mr.
D. G. Rossetti.

A. LANG.

CHAPTER I.

SOME CLASSICAL FORGERIES.

THE practice of writing under the shelter of distinguished names flourished in Greece long even before the zeal of the Ptolemies for their libraries gave it a further stimulus, by the temptation of the good prices they offered for the works of good authors. And further confusion was imported into literature by the custom, in the schools of the sophists, of writing exercises on the imaginary speeches or letters of persons of celebrity: some of which came in time to pass as original works.

It was probably in this way that there came to be composed those Letters of Euripides, of Themistocles, of Socrates, of which Bentley exposed the falsity when he intervened in the literary controversy that raged at the close of the seventeenth century regarding the relative merits of the learning of the ancient and the modern world. But especially successful was he in demonstrating such an origin for the once famous *Letters of Phalaris*. For how could Phalaris, assuming him to have lived in the sixth century B.C., have committed himself to sundry allusions which could only have been possible some centuries later? Anachronisms are the rock on which counterfeit works always run most risk of shipwreck, and it was on this rock that these famous *Letters* of the famous tyrant ultimately perished.

The celebrated controversy which proved thus fatal to the *Letters* is described at length in Bishop Monk's *Life of Bentley* (i., 58-138), and a wonderful controversy it was, leading incidentally to Swift's "Digression Concerning Critics" in the *Tale of a Tub,* and to the "Battle of the Books" (1698). Bentley's overwhelming learning gave him ultimately an easy victory over Charles Boyle and his Christ Church friends ; but now that the dust of the personal quarrel has long been laid to rest, it has to be admitted that Boyle, whose edition of the *Letters* in 1697 gave rise to the controversy, though he believed the *Letters* to be authentic, anticipated Bentley by alluding in his Preface to one point which excited his suspicions of the contrary. He edited them rather as an admirer of their quality than as an out-and-out believer in their genuineness.

A word too may fairly be said on behalf of Sir W. Temple, who, as a champion of the ancients against the moderns, had contended that the oldest books extant were the best of their kind, instancing unfortunately Phalaris and Æsop : the comparative modernity of whom Bentley had little difficulty in establishing. Temple not only thought the *Letters* authentic from the internal evidence, but esteemed them to have "more grace, more spirit, more force of wit and genius, than any others" he had ever seen, either ancient or modern. Bentley on the contrary regarded them as a mere "fardel of common-places, without any life from action or circumstance," and complained of their emptiness and deadness, of their stiffness and operoseness of style. This is to be regretted, as Bentley's verdict has killed the *Letters* for all practical purposes. The last English translation of them was Thomas Francklin's in 1749, and they well deserved translation. For though they may not have the merit of Cicero's, as Bentley said, yet many of them are of uncommon merit. A few to Phalaris' wife Erythia, to his son Paurolas, the letter to the Himeræans about the poet Stesichorus (54), that to Hegesippus on the vanity of public opinion (77), and many others, have in them all the qualities Sir W. Temple affirmed. They might well form part of general classical education, though whether Phalaris was really the affectionate husband, the wise father, the reluctant tyrant, the firm but merciful ruler, the cynical but sensible correspondent, which the *Letters* portray, may well be left among the questions that lie beyond the boundaries of our existing knowledge.

Bentley's criticism was not more fatal to the *Letters of Phalaris* than it was to the fables of Æsop. Yet though all the world knows that the present collection was composed by the Greek poet Babrius, whose age is unknown, and transferred into our present

I *

prose edition by Maximus Palanudes in the fourteenth century, Æsop still holds his rightful place in
every school or nursery of the civilised world.   There
is no reason therefore in the nature of things why Phalaris should be so rigidly excluded.

The actual author of the *Letters of Phalaris* lies
beyond the reach of probable discovery.   And the
same is true of many similar compositions that throng
the classical library.   Bentley never fulfilled his intention of demonstrating the falsity of the Letters
of Democritus, Heraclitus, or Diogenes, which are
contained in the little volume that also has those of
Euripides, but it is doubtless with justice that they
are consigned to one common grave of oblivion.   The
sixty-five letters of Diodorus Siculus, which first
startled the world in 1639, being first printed in
Carrera's *Memorie di Catania*, belong to the same
category.   Nor is it ever likely to be known who
wrote the *Querolus* or *Aulularia* of Plautus, the
Rhesus of Euripides, or the works which tried to
smuggle themselves into notice under such famous
names as those of Plato, Aristotle, and other celeb-
rities.

Some of such works had perhaps at first no
intention of deception, but were mere intellectual
exercises which came from their excellence to pass
as the original works of the authors they imitated :
but the genesis of most lay probably in the quest of
lucre.   In either case the wealth of ability displayed
in their production is amazing, and prevents one from

rejecting as in the nature of things impossible the contention of the Jesuit Hardouin that most of our classical books are monkish forgeries. There are other objections to this conclusion, but no valid objection can be based on the lack of the requisite ability to produce them.

It is, however, only where these classical forgeries are associated with definite names, and assume thereby a kind of personality, that they become of any living interest; and it is only for these, or the most conspicuous of them, that it is here proposed to claim some brief attention. It is curious that the classical writers who have exercised most fascination for the skill of imitators should be Cicero and Petronius Arbiter.

1. Of all the works which the critics have succeeded in condemning to the long catalogue of supposititious works by distinguished writers, none is more remarkable than the so-called *Consolatio* of Cicero; which first saw the light at Venice early in the year 1583, unheralded by a word of explanation regarding its source, and without any hint of a manuscript to support it.

It was known from Cicero's own allusions to the work, and to fragments of it preserved in Lactantius, that, in order to allay in some measure his boundless grief at the loss of his daughter Tullia, Cicero had composed a work of self-consolation, wherein he had condensed all that philosophy could contribute in diminution of his distress. The printed work so nearly approached Cicero in the nobility of its wisdom and the splendour of its language that many at the time accepted it as genuine. It combines the pessimism of Schopenhauer about man's present life with the hopefulness of St. Paul about his future one, and is as well worth reading as many of Cicero's undoubted works. It is to be regretted that to English readers it is still only accessible in Thomas Blacklock's translation, entitled *Paraclesis*, published in 1767, and not very easy to procure.

The book was hardly out before it roused the suspicions of the learned. Antonius Riccobonus, a professor at Padua, was first in the field with a short criticism published in the May of the same year. At a time when imitation of classical authors was more common than it is now, he declared for imitation. Certain passages, he contended, were imitated directly from similar passages in the *Tusculan Disputations*, but expressed in poorer Latin : whilst several words such as "osor" for "qui odit" were declared to be foreign to Cicero's style, and the violation of the Ciceronian rule against a word beginning with N following the word "cum" was pronounced to be a fatal flaw to the title of the new claimant to classical honours.

Thereupon Franciscus Vianelli, who had published the *Consolatio*, wrote to Carlo Sigonio for his opinion. Sigonio distanced all his contemporaries in learning, being then in his fifty-ninth year, and destined to die the year following (1584). In addition to his work as professor at different times at Venice, Padua and Bologna, Sigonio had found time to write in irreproachable Latin historical and other works which fill six large folio volumes.

Sigonio accordingly took up the challenge of his former pupil Riccobonus, and in two famous *Orations* answered all Riccobonus' objections, and successfully disposed of many of them. He tells how on first receiving the work as a gift he regarded it with his customary suspicion, but how on reading it to many listeners he had come round to a contrary opinion, and to a belief that none other than Cicero could have written it (*a nemine alio quam a Tullio scribi dicique potuisse*). If a passage here and there had been added to the text or had been badly expressed, he deprecated on that ground the rejection of the whole work; and he asked, if Cicero had not written it, what living man could have done so in that age.

To this Riccobonus replied in another and amplified criticism, and hazarded the bold conjecture that Sigonio alone of living men had the ability to write like Cicero. Herein he guessed aright, though it was not *proved* for about 200 years. Muratori, in his life of Sigonio, says that he wrote a third oration against his hostile critics, Riccobonus, Gulielmus and Lipsius, and that this treatise, taken to Vianelli to publish, did not appear till 1599, owing to the publisher's wish not to offend Riccobonus, who died in that year. This further defence is probably the treatise called *Accusator* in the sixth volume of Sigonio's works: wherein he marshals the arguments for and against Cicero in a dialogue between an assailant and a defender of his authorship.

In sending his *Orations* to Vianelli at his request, Sigonio pressed Vianelli to disclose the source of the *Consolatio*, and he closed his *Accusator* by the most explicit disclaimer of his own composition of it: "This book I neither wrote, nor published, nor did I instigate any one to publish it". His friend, Antonius Gigantus, the poet, pressed him in vain to acknowledge his authorship, and when he and another after Sigonio's death ransacked his papers, they failed to find the least shred of paper or note bearing on the production of the work.

Sigonio's defence of Cicero was so skilful that many writers hesitated to commit themselves to a belief in Sigonio's authorship. Amongst these was Tiraboschi, the historian of Italian literature. But at last (about 1785) he stumbled upon some original letters from Sigonio to his friend Cammillo Coccupani at Modena, and amongst them was one dated 12th November, 1582, in which Sigonio begged his friend to ask a certain lady whether she had received a letter from him "with a book of mine, *de Consolatione*, which I wrote for her to show to yourself, desiring to have your opinion about it" (*Lett. Ital.*, i., 315, 1787).

Certainly if Sigonio sent his *Consolatio* to a lady to show to a third person, there cannot have been at first much intention of concealment. The conjecture seems therefore plausible that some friend induced him to publish it as Cicero's to see how it would fare at the hands of the learned. At all events Sigonio died without manifesting the smallest desire to undeceive the world about it.

Sigonio's method of construction was most ingenious. A certain passage in Petrarch's *Lettere Senili* (x., 4), in which the poet seeks to console a friend on the loss of a son and grandson, ran as follows :—

"Cum virum tum præcipue senem flere mortalia turpe est, quem tempore et casuum observatione similium contra omnes insultus *obduruisse* (utor peculiaribus meis ac Tullii verbis) atque *occalluisse* conveniat."

Petrarch must have found these two words in some passage of Cicero now lost to us. Sigonio supplied such a passage as follows :—

"Nemo suorum funera experitur, cui non adversa multa antea contigerint : cur igitur graviora, vel certe æque gravia fortiter passus, cum maxime *occalluisse*, et ad dolorem novum *obduruisse* deberet, despondeat animum, seque moerori tradat?"

Sigonio must have composed these words deliberately in order to adapt them to Petrarch's sentiment and to supply the original source of his use of the two rare Ciceronian words.

Sigonio in his defence suggested that Petrarch might at some time have seen the *Consolatio* of Cicero. But unfortunately for this contention Petrarch, who had been the fortunate discoverer of so many of

Cicero's lost works, had never found the *Consolatio*, for in a letter written in the last year of his life (1374) to Luca della Penna he expressly mentions the *Consolatio* as one of the lost works of Cicero for which he had searched in vain (*librum de Consolatione quæsivi anxie nec inveni*).

2. A less successful attempt than that of Sigonio was made to pass as Cicero by some one who published at Bologna in 1811 a fourth book of the *De Natura Deorum*, taking up the subject from the point where the third genuine book had ended. Two years later this work of forty-six pages was reprinted at Oxford by Lunn for the satisfaction of public curiosity, not from any belief that it was other than a forgery.

This little work purported to be edited from a very ancient parchment manuscript. P. Seraphinus, Ord. Fr. Min., professed to have found it in a certain shop among sundry books bought at an auction, and to have been allowed to take away the torn and worm-eaten document. He had resolved to print it in order to show the similarity of its doctrines to those of the Catholic Church; the editor being convinced that, had Cicero been born in the Christian era, he would have conformed to the orthodox faith. And lest any one should think that Seraphinus himself had composed the work, he swore most solemnly by St. Francis d'Assisi that of such a composition he was quite incapable: which may have been true as regarded a friar of wholly fictitious existence.

But the writer went too far with his Christianity of Cicero, nor could the undoubted cleverness of his production save a work which put into the mouth of Cicero expressions that presupposed a knowledge of St. Paul. Not only is Cicero made to use a word so foreign to his style or his time as the word *religiositas* for "a sense of religion," but he is made to apply to the Athenians the epithet St. Paul applied to them (δεισιδαιμονέστατοι), "too much given to religion". He speaks of "revelation" (*revelatio*) and "the infallible rule of faith," like any Christian, and indulges in utterances so remarkable as :—

"There is no salvation (*salus*) save in the communion with the universality of the saints, save in the common family of the faithful" (*fidei addictorum*) (c. 52).

Or again he speaks of it as the first principle of religion "to acquiesce in those things, to approve and to conform to that which has been believed always, and in all places, and by all men, or at least by most" (c. 13).

And finally Cicero deduces a universal terrestrial monarchy from the celestial, and asks, as an advocate for the temporal power of the Pope, "To what other seat save that of Rome could that supreme pontificate more fitly appertain?"

In his quite ultramontane Christianity he even anticipates the Pope's infallibility: "By the common consent of all men the supreme Roman Pope (*pontifex*) of Rome is of right the sovereign in matters of religion . . . who cannot be wrong or err in anything pertaining to religion ".

This is all ridiculous enough, good and Ciceronian as was the Latin in which this hoax was perpetrated. The motive and the personality of the perpetrator are alike obscure. At one time it was attributed to Philipp Marheinecke or to De Wette, both Protestant theologians ; but subsequently these writers were acquitted, and the blame has since oscillated between Cludius and Buckholz (Græsse's *Tresor des Livres Rares*, ii., 172). By Cludius of Heidelberg must be meant Hermann Heimart Cludius of Hildesheim, born in 1754, and for fifty years (1787 to 1827) superintendent of the Church of St. George's at Hildesheim. *Wolff's Encyclopedia* attributes to him the composition of fourteen works, poetical, philosophical and theological ; but neither his works, his profession, nor his position seem easily consistent with his composition of a forgery. Whether there is any better reason to connect Buckholz with the work is not apparent, and it must remain a mystery for what reason common conjecture pitched upon Protestant theologians as the likeliest authors of a work that sought to identify Cicero with the tenets of ultramontane Catholicism.

3. The history of literature is strewn with the reputations of the learned, who have either wrongly doubted or wrongly believed. And often no decisive victory has declared itself for either combatant, and legitimate doubt has survived an accepted armistice.

This is well illustrated by the case of the Trau fragment of the famous *Satyricon*, ascribed to Petronius, the friend, the minister, and finally the victim of Nero.

The first printed edition of Petronius appeared in Venice in 1499, and consisted of only thirty-eight pages. With this sorry and almost sole remnant of Roman fiction the world had to content itself for about a century and a half, although quotations from it in the *Polycraticus* of John of Salisbury, the English Bishop of Chartres, proved a knowledge of a more complete work existent in the twelfth century.

Then came a find, round which still hangs considerable mystery. In a library said to belong to Nicholas Cippicus at Trau, in Dalmatia, in a volume containing also manuscript copies of Catullus, Tibullus and Propertius, was discovered by Marinus Statileus, on his return from the completion of his law studies at Padua, that additional episode in the Petronian story which is known as the " Supper of Trimalchio," referred to by John of Salisbury.

The fullest contemporary account of this find is that given by John Lucius in his *Memorie Istoriche di Tragurio* (Trau) in 1674. Statileus brought the manuscript he had found to Lucius, himself a native of Trau, and Lucius urged him to print it just as it was "for the honour of the country" (*per decoro della patria*). But he could not prevail, and, leaving Trau in 1654, Lucius told certain learned men in Padua and Rome of the discovery, and vainly exhorted Statileus and Cippicus to have it printed (531).

This proves that the manuscript was found some time before 1654, a much earlier date than is usually supposed. And it must have been discovered much earlier still, for Dr. Spon found Statileus a man of nearly sixty in 1675. It was between 1639 and 1645 that Statileus can be proved to have been at Padua, so that he must have found the manuscript about the year 1645, which would leave some twenty years between its discovery and its first printed appearance in 1664. This is highly incredible, and even ten years is a long time to allow for the conquest by Lucius of the modesty or the indolence of his friend and relative Statileus.

The licence to publish the discovery is dated 2nd December, 1663, at Padua, and in the year following it was published both at Padua and at Paris, the same preface being prefixed to both editions. This preface gives the story of Statileus finding it in the Cippican Library, and of his taking counsel about it with the learned men of Venice and Holland and more especially with John Rhodius, who died at Rome in 1659. Statileus here takes the place subsequently claimed by Lucius himself in the matter of consulting the learned world. Statileus, after pressure from the Venetian ambassador at Rome, had readily agreed to send a copy of the manuscript to Rome for examination, after which Frambotti at Padua, having obtained it from Statileus, offered it to the perusal of the public in the exact form in which he had received it from Statileus (*nudum et quale ab eodem impetratum accepimus*).

This edition, though it had been thus submitted to the approval of the learned (*doctissimi cujusque in urbe censuræ subjectus liber*), was full of the most astounding words and phrases. And in March, 1665, the erudite Frenchman, Adrian de Valois, boldly declared that every page of it bore palpable marks of forgery and imposture. Such monstrous words abounded in it that, if Petronius wrote them, Petronius must have been ignorant of Latin. Genders, cases and declensions were all hopelessly wrong, and the incidents of the feast clashed at many points with Roman customs. It was to be rejected as wholly ridiculous.

It was a strong case that he made. And he was supported by a younger critic, a German, called Wagenseil, who unhesitatingly pronounced it a forgery. Many of its words were more than barbarous; they were not even human. The work was clearly a very recent abortion by some miserable man (*inepti alicujus homuncionis*), and he would fain whisper to Statileus that he was himself the man, and that he would do wisely to make a clean breast of it.

A vigorous reply to these critics appeared forthwith, called the *Responsio* (1666). It professed to be by Marinus Statileus of Trau, a jurisconsult, and many bad points made by Wagenseil it answered completely. But though contemporaries accepted it as by Statileus, it was only written *for* Statileus, not *by* him, as was pretended, nor is it certain by whom it was written.　Lucius some years later said that he was told by Michel Antonius Baudrand of Paris that the famous Dr. Peter Petit of Paris, whom Lucius had known at Rome, was its real composer (*Memoirs of Trau*, p. 532); and it may be that this suggestion is the source of the ascription of the *Responsio* to Petit by his friend the Abbé Nicaise in the long list of that versatile writer's works in his *Epistola de obitu Petri Petiti* (in 1698).　Petit therefore may have written it, but there is no clear proof, and the tradition that he did write it is probably responsible for the erroneous statement by many subsequent writers that Petit was the actual discoverer of the manuscript.

At all events the dispute about its authenticity led at last to the sending of the actual manuscript to Rome, where in August, 1668, a meeting of experts is said to have assigned it, from the similarity of the writing and paper to those of an original work of Petrarch, an antiquity of 300 years (Goujet, *Bib. Franc.*, i., 212).　Their verdict may be read at length in Lucius' *Memoirs of Trau* (533), copied verbatim from the *Giornale dei Letterati* for 27th August, 1668 : an ecclesiastical periodical which unfortunately omits to give us the names of the experts.

In November of that same year we find a letter from Lucius to the brothers Blaeu, the publishers, at Amsterdam (14th November, 1668), wherein he alludes to his having often inspected and read the

manuscript at Trau (that is, before 1654); to his
having shown it to the brothers themselves when at
Rome; and to his efforts to overcome Statileus' unaccountable reluctance to publish the work.   He
sends them a copy from which to print a fresh edition,
and at the same time he sends them a fresh defence
of it by Statileus.   This defence must have been the
Apologia which was published in 1669; and which
purported, like the *Responsio*, to be by Statileus,
being addressed by him facetiously to "the Conscript
Fathers of the Literary Commonwealth".

As the *Responsio* was attributed to Petit, it was
only natural that the *Apologia* should be attributed
to him also, though for this there is not even the
authority of Lucius, who most distinctly assigns it to
his friend, the Abbé Gradi, the librarian of the Vatican
(*Memoirs of Trau*, p. 535).   Why he should do so
is not clear, seeing that he had himself sent it to the
Blaeu brothers as being the work of Statileus.   And
here appears a remarkable thing: there is strong
internal evidence that Lucius had a hand in it himself.   Adrian de Valois had spoken slightingly of
the town of Trau, and accordingly in reply to him
the author of the *Apologia* breaks out towards the
end into a long and rather irrelevant eulogy of this
place.   Its antiquity is traced back to Dionysius of
Syracuse, 2,000 years before; the allusions to it by
Strabo and Polybius are referred to; and a summary
is given of its history.   No Parisian, like Petit,
would have launched out into this eulogy of Trau,

2

nor have possessed the knowledge requisite for such
a task.   It must have come from some native of
Trau, such as was Lucius himself.   And if we turn
to the first book of his *Memoirs of Trau* we there
actually find in Italian precisely the same history of
Trau that we find in Latin in the *Apologia;* there
are the same allusions to Dionysius of Syracuse,
380 years B.C. ; to Strabo and Polybius; the same
pride in the antiquity of Trau.   But what is still
more remarkable, the *Apologia* ends its eulogy of
Trau by an allusion to its utter destruction by the
Saracens : a fact which is also told in the *Memoirs*,
but is there told as resting solely on the authority
of an Archdeacon Tregnano, a writer whom Lucius
had recovered from oblivion.   Lucius, it is true, had
mentioned the fact in his book on the *History of Dalmatia*, published in 1666, and as Gradi had himself
licensed this book on behalf of the Index he might in
this way have acquired the information ; but its more
probable connexion with Lucius is confirmed by the
very language of the two passages.

When therefore we find these facts : Lucius sending the *Apologia* to the publishers as the work of
Statileus ; these publishers remaining in such ignorance of the truth that in a second edition of it in
1671 they still refer to Statileus as its author ; then
in 1674 Lucius openly assigning it to Gradi, who
was alive to contradict it ; and the strong internal
evidence withal that no one but Lucius himself could
have written at least some part of it ; suspicion can-

not but arise that Lucius had some motive for all this mystification, and that some underground work in connection with the "Supper of Trimalchio" must be divided between himself, Gradi, and Statileus or Statilius. One is driven back to the suspicion, which Wagenseil never surrendered, that after all the "Supper of Trimalchio" may be a forgery.

But is not the manuscript its own evidence? Is it not in the National Library at Paris (Lat. 7989), and did it not pass the close scrutiny of experts at Rome in 1668?

But was it ever said who these experts were? Did they include Gradi and Lucius amongst them? And how comes it that these experts ascribed it to the age of Petrarch (who died 1374), when Dr. Spon in 1675 found the date of 20th November, 1423, inscribed on one of the pages? Either this addition was made in the interval, or by a miraculous blindness the experts overlooked it. But the addition seems more probable than the blindness.

Dr. Spon found the manuscript in the library of Marinus Statileus, who might, he thought, have told him more about it but for some illness which then affected him. Eleven years later the Père Mabillon saw the same manuscript at Modena in the library of Laurence, the son of Marinus (Menagiana, iii., 205, from Mabillon's *Iter Italicum*, 202). But the Père Montfaucon, who actually bought it for France, knows nothing of this sojourn at Modena. His story is that, after the death of Statileus, it fell into

the hands of a Dalmatian who brought it to Rome
in the hope thereby to advance his fortunes.   Being
disappointed in this, and in want of money, he pawned
it to Peter Paul Mariano, and, when he came to repay the money, still left the Codex with Mariano.
The Abbé de Louvois would have bought it from
Mariano for the Royal Library, had not the price
asked for it brought the negotiation to an end.   On
Mariano's death Montfaucon, by the help of a friend,
bought it on reasonable terms from Mariano's heirs
(*Bibliotheca Bibliothecarum*, ii., 758).   So it found its
way to Paris.

Montfaucon twice gives the year 1703 as that in
which he bought the manuscript, but Menage, who
died in 1692, is made to speak of having seen it in the
Royal Library and to have recognised it as genuine
at least twelve years before it can have been there
at all (Menagiana, iii., 205)!

But doubtless the manuscript which Montfaucon
bought is the same which Spon saw in 1675.   The
volume contains Tibullus, Propertius, Catullus and
" The Supper," and Montfaucon vouches for all these
having been written by the same hand.

A later and better description of the Codex is
given in Beck's *Manuscripts of the Satyricon* (1863).
" The Supper " begins on page 206 of the small
leather-bound folio.   The first three pages are much
paler than the rest ; " they seem to have suffered
from exposure, rubbing, or other causes ".   On page
209 is a change to a darker ink, to larger letters, and

to fewer lines to the page. Still Beck thought there was the same handwriting throughout, though his allusions to rubbings and to different inks do not tend to allay suspicion, as these are not unknown as among the indications of literary trickery.

With these suspicious antecedents literature became possessed of that specimen of almost impossible Latin, known as the "Supper of Trimalchio". That John of Salisbury referred to this supper in his *Polycraticus* (iv., 5, and viii., 7) does not of itself prove the genuineness of the Trau fragment. In any case that fragment left the *Satyricon* obviously incomplete, and gave scope for further discoveries. Nor was it long before another was made.

4. This was the discovery claimed by Francis Nodot, who combined the profession of arms with no small skill in letters. On 12th October, 1690, he wrote an ecstatic letter to M. Charpentier, then Director of the French Academy, announcing his discovery of the remainder of Petronius. His story was that after having heard from a German that a certain M. Dupin, a French officer in the service of the Emperor of Austria in the campaign against Turkey, had become possessed of such a manuscript at the siege of Belgrade, he had succeeded by the help of a Frankfurt merchant in obtaining from M. Dupin a copy of the manuscript. No one but the shadowy M. Dupin ever saw the manuscript, but the copy was published at Rotterdam in 1693 as the complete work of Petronius, the additional words and para-

graphs being printed in a different type from those
of the work as hitherto known, and every Latin page
being accompanied on the opposite one with a French
translation.   The additional matter in prose and
verse did not amount to very much in quantity, but
the work speedily acquired popularity, and was translated into English in 1694, and again in 1708, and
this latter translation by Mr. Wilson and others of
the Middle Temple was reprinted verbatim in 1899
for private circulation only, but with no publisher's
name on the title-page.

On 9th November, 1690, M. Charpentier congratulated Nodot on his discovery, but a goodly
battle was in store also for this version of Petronius.
The critics, again repelled by many Gallic and barbarous words, took most offence at the use of the
word *castellum* (translated into French as *château*),
for a " country house," at a time long prior to the existence of such *châteaux*.   Many of the phrases in the
new fragments were shown to be taken from phrases
in the real Petronius, and many of the corrections
and conjectures of the commentators were found to be
embodied in the text of the new version.   Also the
story of the smith who invented unbreakable glass
agreed verbally with John of Salisbury's extract
from the " Supper of Trimalchio," instead of with the
abbreviated form of the same story as given in the
Trau fragment.   Twelve Latin verses also came
straight from John of Salisbury, and there were
many indications of the whole work having been

pieced together from various sources with no small expenditure of ingenuity. The best account of this adverse criticism is that given by Gachet d'Artigny in his *Nouveaux Mémoires d'histoire* (i., 346-76, 1749).

Bentley, in an *obiter dictum*, alluded in 1697 to Nodot's version as a "bungling supplement," and as a "scandal to all forgeries". And so the verdict has remained, despite the *Contre-Critique* which in 1700 Nodot published in defence of his Petronius, and in which he successfully answered several of the weaker objections of his adversaries. His appeal to the case of the Trau fragment, which after similar objections to those raised against his own version had been passed as genuine by the critics, was not without force; but in the case of his version he should have remembered that no one but himself had ever seen so much of the original as the alleged transcript by the alleged M. Dupin. The Trau manuscript had a real existence.

It would be natural to ascribe the deception in this case to Nodot himself. But his belief in the genuineness of his Petronius has little appearance of simulation, and his anxiety to consult learned men and academies about the merits of the work seems an indication of his good faith in the matter. It is also open to doubt whether he had the requisite ability for the task of a forger. A contemporary, who knew him in 1706 engaged at Lille in the provisioning department of the army, described him to

Gachet d'Artigny as not at all the kind of man to be capable of imitating Petronian Latin. To meet the difficulty the suggestion was made by Petrequin that the actual composition was the work of Linage de Vauciennes, who is known to have translated the *Satyricon* into French and to have filled the gaps with his own invention, and that he was aided by the notorious Nicholas Chorier, who perhaps lent it to Nodot. Chorier died in 1692, and in this direction may lie the solution of the puzzle. Quérard called it an ingenious conjecture, and beyond that it seems impossible to advance (*Supercheries Littéraires*, Petronius).

5. The last attempt to hoax the world with Petronius was that of the Spaniard, Joseph Marchena, who in 1800 published a fragment of Petronius purporting to be extracted from a very ancient manuscript found in the monastery of St. Gallen in Switzerland, and accompanied by a French translation and notes, by " Lallemandus sacræ theologiæ doctor ". As a matter of fact the notes were the primary object of the work, the text being produced afterwards as a peg whereon to hang them. The text consisted of only a few pages, but they were so deftly fitted in to the real text of Petronius and so skilfully imitative of his style that many learned men in Germany were deceived by it. Marchena, who became a naturalised Frenchman after fear of the Inquisition had driven him from Spain, was secretary to General Moreau during his campaign on the Rhine; and it seems to have been in

answer to a sort of challenge from the general that he attempted his task. He seems not to have intended anything more than a hoax. But its success led him later to pretend to having found among the ruins of Herculaneum forty unpublished verses of Catullus, though in this case the Germans had the laugh at him. Marchena is described as a dwarf, of deformed and repulsive appearance, who fancied his attractions irresistible to the other sex, and who ultimately died in great poverty. His "fragment" is a terrible production, but it serves to illustrate the possibility of so cleverly imitating ancient writers as to deceive the very elect among the moderns. If Petronius was so imitable in the nineteenth century, why should he have been less so in the seventeenth?

CHAPTER II.

BERTRAM: "THE PAUSANIAS OF BRITAIN".

FEW literary frauds have ever been committed more extraordinary than that which the criticism of the learned has, not without strong opposition, laid to the charge of Charles Julius Bertram. For no reasonable motive, pecuniary or other, has ever been or can be assigned for his conduct, and at the best we are asked to choose between vanity and insanity as his guiding principle.

Bertram's father was a silk dyer, who migrated from England with his family to Copenhagen in the year 1743, and the year following set up as a hosier. Charles Julius, the son, born in 1723, must have then been in his twenty-first year. In July, 1747, though belonging to the Anglican Church, his petition to become a student at the university was granted, and in that capacity he acquired the friendship and patronage of Gramm, the privy-councillor and chief librarian to the King of Denmark. Subsequently Bertram became Professor of English in the Royal Marine Academy at Copenhagen, and a Danish-English grammar is one among many other testimonies to his industry and ability in the field of learning.

In 1747 he began a correspondence with the celebrated English antiquary, Dr. Stukeley, who says : "In the summer of 1747, 11th June, whilst I lived at Stamford, I received a letter from Charles Julius Bertram, Professor of the English tongue in the Royal Marine Academy of Copenhagen ". Inasmuch, however, as Bertram only became a student in July of 1747, he cannot have been a professor in the June of that year ; and this has been urged against him as a falsehood. But Stukeley nowhere says that Bertram so described himself, and the passage quoted may only refer to Bertram's position at that later date when Stukeley was narrating his transactions with him.

A correspondence between Bertram and Stukeley ensued, in the course of which Bertram referred to a curious manuscript history of Roman Britain by Richard of Westminster which he had seen in the possession of a friend. Stukeley for some time thought no more of the matter, but ended by writing for an extract from the manuscript. An imitation having been sent, and pronounced by the Keeper of the Cotton Library to be 400 years old, Stukeley became more interested, and begged Bertram, if he could, to get possession of the manuscript ; this being with difficulty accomplished, he solicited a transcript of the whole, and a copy of the map that went with it. This transcript reached him in a succession of letters, and Stukeley, deeming it "the greatest treasure we could now boast of in this kind of learning," pressed Bertram to print it; a request with which Bertram complied in 1757, when he published his alleged discovery in the little volume called *Britannicarum Gentium Historiæ Antiquæ Scriptores tres: Ricardus Corinensis, Gildas Badonicus, Nennius Banchorensis.* The original title of the single history was *Ricardi monachi Westmonasteriensis commentariolum geographicum, de Situ Britanniæ, et stationum quas in ea insula Romani ædificaverunt.*

It appears that there really was a monk of Westminster between the years 1450 and 1472 called Richard, but Stukeley insisted that this could not be the Richard in question, and suggested that the real writer was another monk of Westminster, the better known Richard of Cirencester, who flourished a century earlier.

To this suggestion of superior wisdom Bertram bowed, speaking of his treatise as *believed* to have been written by Richard of Cirencester. Thereby he exposed himself to needless difficulties, for the frequent references to classical authors, which have been urged as highly improbable in a monk of the fourteenth century, would be less improbable in any writer towards the end of the fifteenth. And the faults of Latin and variations of words which distinguish the treatise from the sole surviving Latin work of Richard of Cirencester could not have been objected against a work by Richard of Westminster who had left no such standard of literary comparison behind him.

Stukeley's reasons for ascribing the work to Richard of Cirencester are quite insufficient and fanciful. Richard of Cirencester had travelled much, visited libraries, and written books ; therefore he, and no later Richard, must have written the *De Situ*. Had Bertram not acceded to this bad logic, many of the reasons for denouncing the *De Situ* a forgery would have been non-existent.

It is to be regretted that the letters about the manuscript between Stukeley and Bertram, covering a space of two years, are no longer available to shed light on the story. In 1847 Bertram's letters to Stukeley were in the possession of Mr. John Britton, the antiquary, who intended at one time to present them to the British Museum, but who unfortunately never did so, though possibly they somewhere exist. It is consequently impossible to judge of the amount of discretion shown by Stukeley in his dealing with Bertram.

It is common to write of Stukeley as a man of vanity, and a ready dupe to any knave who came by. But he appears to have acted with reasonable prudence. It was not till 18th March, 1756, after a period of nine years for correspondence, for conversation, for consideration about the manuscript, that he read before the Antiquarian Society his *Account of Richard of Cirencester, Monk of Westminster, and of his*

Works : an account which he published the year
following (1757), when Bertram also published his
work, and which he dedicated to the President of the
Society, Lord Willoughby of Parham.   With an air
of triumph at his good fortune in having saved " this
most invaluable work" of Richard of Cirencester,
Stukeley proceeds to relate all he had been able to
collect concerning that worthy, and in what manner
he had become acquainted with the work through
Bertram.   He also tells us much about the map which
accompanied Richard's treatise, and which he prefixed
to his published *Account*, and adds a transcript of the
curious *Itinerary* of Richard, and an alphabetical list
of the Roman names of places with his best conjectures as to their modern equivalents.

Much that Richard told of the ancient Britons,
of their manners and military institutions, and of the
Druids, was borrowed from Cæsar, but it was the
new information contained in the book which chiefly
commended it to Stukeley.   More than a hundred
names of cities, roads, and people were added to our
knowledge of Roman Britain ; the province of Ves-
pasiana was added to the five previously known ; and
the Roman dominion was shown to have extended
as far as Inverness.   Englishmen learnt with pride
how the natives of Surrey (the Senones) had crossed
the Alps under Brennus, and besieged and wasted
Rome.   Though many of the journeys across Britain
coincided with those of Antoninus' *Itinerary*, they
were not copied from that source, which Stukeley

vouched for it that Richard had never seen. Many
facts were also added to the history of Britain concerning the expeditions of emperors and legates,
the taking of cities, the emigration to Ireland, the
building of the walls, and a persecution of the Christians which involved an increase of 17,000 to the
army of martyrs. And the whole was written "with
great judgment, perspicuity, and conciseness, as by
one that was altogether master of his subject". No
wonder that Stukeley was proud of his discovery,
which extended beyond all expectation the knowledge of the past history of his country. In a letter
to Dr. Mead (27th March, 1749) he terminated his
account of Richard by calling him "the Pausanias of
Britain".

This interesting work of Richard or of Bertram
is best read, in English, in Giles' *Six Old English
Chronicles* (1848), or in its Latin original, in the
Description of Britain, published anonymously by
Hatcher, the historian of Salisbury, in 1809. The
work is a mosaic of information collected from Cæsar,
Tacitus, Selinus, Camden, and other authorities, about
early Britain; the author not concealing his indebted-
ness to these previous writers, but incorporating many
passages from them without any indication that such
passages were quotations. It is certain from Bertram's preface and notes to his *Tres Scriptores* that
he was well read in all that related to the antiquities
of Britain, and it must be supposed that he amused
his leisure by utilising his knowledge for the produc-

tion of his extremely clever compilation. In the
library of Corpus Christi College, at Cambridge,
there is a manuscript ascribed to Bede, which has
never been published, entitled "De Situ Britanniæ
et de mirabilibus ejus". It is curious that the former
part of the title should be identical with that of the
work ascribed to Richard. That Bertram knew of it
is evident from his suggestion in his preface that it
ought to be published, but it is fair to wonder how
he knew of it, and whether he had ever seen it.

The havoc that Bertram's fraud (if such it was)
played with our history is difficult to realise. Though
some writers were doubtful or cautious about quoting
his authority, the majority reposed on him gladly.
Especially was this the case with county historians,
of whom a complete survey is given in Mr. Mayor's
preface to his edition of Richard de Cirencester's
Speculum Historiale de gestis rerum Angliæ. For
example: "This valuable work and more valuable
map . . . containing the best and largest account of
Britannia Romana yet extant" (Hutchin's *Hist. of
Dorset*, i., 16).

"That the work is genuine," wrote the antiquary,
J. Whitaker, "needs no proof. All the embodied
antiquarians of the fourteenth and three succeeding
centuries could not have forged so learned a detail of
Roman antiquities" (*Hist. of Manchester*, i., 54).
Many pages of this kind are quoted by Mr. Mayor.

Even the great Gibbon himself escaped not altogether from Bertram ; and readers of that immortal

historian must revise their idea of early Britain contained in such a passage as the following : " Under the protection of the Romans ninety-two considerable towns had arisen in the several parts of that great province, and among these thirty-three cities were distinguished among the rest by their superior privileges and importance " (c. 31). This and other details about the constitution of Roman Britain Gibbon borrows entirely from Richard, adding the remark that "although it may not seem probable that he wrote from the MSS. of a Roman general, he shows a genuine knowledge of antiquity very extraordinary for a monk of the fourteenth century ".

It is not too much to say that the pseudo-Richard has entered deeply into the mental equipment of most Englishmen. How could it be otherwise when from such a source the Ordnance Survey derived the names of Roman stations for its maps, and scholastic geographical works borrowed from it with implicit trust for the instruction of the young? It is impossible to gauge the influence which this probable fiction still exercises indirectly on our notions of England in Roman times.

From an early date many regarded the whole composition as a hoax, but opinion oscillated fairly evenly between belief and disbelief, till in 1845 Karl Wex, a German writer, vigorously challenged its authenticity, and turned the scale in favour of incredulity. He showed how the quotations from

Tacitus were taken from recent editions, which lay obviously beyond the knowledge of any monks of Westminster. For example, the oldest editions of Tacitus in *Agricola*, 16, had the words *cognito provinciæ motu*; the Venetian edition of 1497 had by mistake *co cognito*, which, as impossible, later editors altered to *eo cognito*. Richard too had *eo cognito*. But how or why in the fourteenth century? The reply, that Bertram, in copying the MS., improved on it by adopting these later readings, could hardly be considered convincing.

Many other objections have been raised against the manuscript. Its Latinity has been described by Mr. Woodward as having "the flavour of a public school exercise very badly done," and it is very dissimilar in vocabulary and phraseology to Richard of Cirencester's surviving and genuine work, the *Speculum Historiale*. It is, however, a curious coincidence that both the *Speculum* and the *De Situ* open with the same allusion to Britain having been originally called Albion. The *Speculum* begins: "Post primum insulæ Britanniæ regem nomine Brutum (a quo dicta insula *quæ prius Albion vocabatur*)". The *De Situ* begins its second paragraph with: "Veteres Britanniam ab albis rupibus *primum Albionem*, postea vocabulo gentis suæ Britanniam cognominaverunt".

But more remarkable than this coincidence between the real and the alleged Richard is the following coincidence between the supposed Richard and Bertram. For Bertram in the preface to his publication addressed his work "Candido et *Benevolo lectori*," an appeal to the "kind reader" which came naturally enough from a writer in the eighteenth century. But was such an appeal a common literary habit in the fourteenth or fifteenth century? It is surely something more than a coincidence that the supposed monk should, towards the close of his first book, commend it to the "kind reader" (*Benevolo lectori*), precisely as Bertram commended his book several centuries later. Was not one and the same mind behind the same phrase in each instance?

But the greatest difficulty about Bertram's discovery lay in the fact that the manuscript of Richard's *De Situ* had never been seen by any one. Stukeley, in his correspondence with Bertram, expressed the natural desire that, if possible, the manuscript original should be purchased for the British Museum, but to this suggestion Bertram would not listen. It was suggested that Bertram's friend, who was said to own the MS., had been wild in his youth, and stolen the document from a volume in some English library. Not long after Bertram's death in January, 1765, at the age of forty-three, inquiries were made about the MS., but Lord Spencer's search for it at Copenhagen, and all other efforts to find it proving unavailing, the inference has been naturally drawn that its non-existence accounted for its non-discovery. The inference, however, does not amount to proof, considering with what facility a manuscript is lost or destroyed, and

3 *

also the fact that the MS., if it existed, never belonged
to Bertram.

A more convincing argument against the manuscript lies in the small specimen of it which Bertram
sent to Stukeley and of which that antiquarian printed
a facsimile at the end of his *Account of Richard*.
It may also be seen in the frontispiece of Mr. Mayor's
preface.   It has been declared by Mr. Woodward,
the Librarian of Windsor Castle, to bear no resemblance to the handwriting of the fourteenth or indeed
of any century, "and to be plainly a clumsy forgery
by an unpractised hand, not a tracing or copy from
a genuine original".   Some of the letters have strange
unusual terminals, and others are dissimilar from those
in Richard's genuine writing.   But two curious facts
must be remembered about it : (1) that when Stukeley showed it to his friend, Mr. Caseley, the Keeper
of the Cotton Library, that gentleman immediately
pronounced it to be 400 years old ; (2) that about
the year 1840 Sir F. Madden in the manuscript department of the British Museum showed Mr. Wright
a facsimile of these same lines in a letter from Bertram to Stukeley, and pointed out a number of minute
characteristics in the writing, which led him to believe it a genuine product of the fourteenth century.
At the same time Sir F. Madden animadverted on
the rashness of the Council of the Historical Society
in having decided to reject Richard from their series
of our early historians (*Literary Gazette* for 11th
July, 1846).

There were few, if any, better palæographists in his time than Sir F. Madden, and, whether or not he came to revise his opinion, the fact that he at one time accepted this sample of the MS. as genuine must in fairness be set against the judgment of Mr. Woodward. If the Keeper of the manuscript department of the British Museum, and the Keeper of the Cotton Library, could so easily be deceived by a forgery, of what value is expert opinion? We are left without a compass on a sea of doubt.

The balance of argument is against Bertram. But the fact that his Itineraries supply some Roman roads and stations, unrecorded by other writers, which have been identified by modern antiquaries, can only be accounted for at the expense either of the ability or of the veracity of those antiquaries. Of the ability and knowledge displayed by him there can be no question. One is astonished that so much learning and skill should have gone to a mere fabrication. And if the object was the amusement of deceiving Stukeley, the joke can have had little zest, seeing that Stukeley went to his grave without a suspicion of the deceit that had been practised on him. The total absence for any assignable motive for a forgery would, in default of counter reasons, supply a strong argument in favour of Bertram.

Nothing known of his life or character or company would of itself lend any support to suspicion of his literary honesty. During and after his connexion with Stukeley he was occupied with works which

would seem to indicate a temperament far removed
from the disposition one would expect in a forger.
Two years after the announcement of his great
discovery we find him publishing an *Essay on the
Excellency of the English Tongue* (1749); then the
Rudimenta Grammaticæ Anglicanæ (1750); the next
year *Ethics from various Authors* (1751); two years
later his *Royal English-Danish Grammar* (1753);
seven years later he translates into Danish an English
work *On the Great Advantages of a Godly Life*
(1760); whilst his last work is a *Statistical Account
of the Danish Army* (1762). Three years later he
died (1765), leaving an unblemished reputation, and
his great addition to the history and literature of
England neither challenged nor suspected.

So far as passing off on the world a fictitious
composition was concerned, he was completely successful. No suspicion or fear of detection appears to
have haunted him; the taint on his fame was posthumous. Nor was discovery, when it came, of that
conclusive kind which convinces everybody; many
distinguished authorities believed in his story, and
not a few believe in it still. If their faith has survived
the perusal of Mr. Mayor's preface, nothing is ever
likely to disturb it. But some mystery still attaches
to the story.

CHAPTER III.

GREEK FORGERY: CONSTANTINE SIMONIDES.

OF all the names which belong to the darker side of literature none is more famous or interesting than that of Constantine Simonides, the Greek, who claims the year 1820 as that of his birth. For with whatever right Simonides is assigned to the forging fraternity, his industry, his learning, and his adventures claim for him a position apart, whilst it may be doubted whether any of his contemporaries in the learned world at all approached him in the art of calligraphy or in his knowledge of palæography.

And it may be questioned whether the world is yet right as to the truth or falsity of all the claims of Simonides. The received theory about him, that he made use of genuine MSS. as a cloak to palm off spurious documents, is open to the objection that it was on the occasion of his *first* visit to Sir Frederick Madden at the British Museum that he offered documents, all of which Sir Frederick refused as spurious, and that it was on the day following that he brought another supply, all of which Sir Frederick bought for the nation as genuine, and which are included between the numbers 19386 and 19393 in the Additional MSS. of the Museum. This was in February, 1853. In this transaction, as described by Sir Frederick himself, it is clear that the genuine documents were in no sense used as a means to facilitate the passing of forgeries ; the forgeries, if such they were, being offered first.

The manuscripts bought as genuine by the Museum are beautiful specimens of writing on vellum, and belong to any century from the tenth to the fifteenth. The other vellum documents which Sir F. Madden rejected as spurious were with some others soon afterwards sold to that great collector of manuscripts, Sir Thomas Phillipps, who amassed his huge collection of 60,000 manuscripts on the principle that it was better to buy even a forgery than to let pass a MS. that might be genuine. In the list of thirty-one documents which he bought of Simonides (and some of them for no mean sums) he distinguished in a letter to the *Athenæum* (4th February, 1857) between those he thought genuine and those he thought forgeries. Some he thought had been dipped in tobacco-water to give them the semblance of age. Others, rejected by Sir F. Madden, he accepted as genuine ; the three first books of the *Iliad*, for instance, on a thin vellum roll in extremely diminutive letters he declared to be, if a forgery, "the most wonderful and successful attempt ever accomplished ". And so he thought of the Anacreon and of the Hesiod. And with him will surely agree all whom

curiosity leads to inspect these literary marvels, now
in the possession of Mr. Fitzroy Fenwick at Thirle-
staine House in Cheltenham.   It is wholly incredible that Simonides should have been at the
trouble of forging these works.   It may not have
been beyond his power to produce some or all of
them in their different handwritings; but some of
them are of great length, No. 13865 consisting of 567
pages, No. 13866 of 770, and it is far less likely
that he forged these books than that he acquired
them, as he said, from the monasteries on Mount
Athos, where he resided for many months about the
year 1840.

As illustrating the uncertainty of the distinction
between genuine and spurious, it must be noted that
all these MSS., those accepted by Sir F. Madden and
those bought by Sir T. Phillipps, had been shown at
Athens in 1848, and the result of two Commissions,
appointed by the Government to examine them, were
on the whole but not decisively adverse to their
authenticity.   The Homer was said to show striking
resemblances to a recent foreign edition of that bard;
but it is so highly illegible that it is fair to doubt
whether any one ever really read it through.   In
1851 Mr. Rancabes, the Greek poet, condemned all
Simonides' MSS. as forgeries, in the *Pandora;* he
thought they all bore traces of having been composed by one hand, and he calculated that the whole
collection might have been produced in about a year
and a half.   But there was strong political antagon-

ism between Rancabes and Simonides, and this probably coloured the criticism. In any case the verdict
of Rancabes had no influence on Sir F. Madden,
whose judgment was at least unaffected by political
bias.

And it is in favour of the genuineness of most of
Sir Thomas' purchases that their titles and the
names of their authors correspond with works which
still exist in the monasteries of Mount Athos, whence
Simonides professed to have derived them. Both
classical and ecclesiastical works of the same name
and character as those which figure among Sir
Thomas' purchases abound in Professor Lampros'
recent Catalogue of all the manuscripts of all the
monasteries on Mount Athos, and Simonides had
abundant opportunities of acquiring or copying such
works during the period when he was first resident on
Mount Athos, between 1839 and 1841, and again in
1852. In the case of these MSS. the forgery, if such
there was, cannot be clearly traced to him, for he may
himself have become the innocent possessor of spurious works. He sold, for instance, to Sir Thomas
three Chrusobulls or Golden Bulls of the Emperors ;
Professor Lampros, in a recent account of the monasteries, speaks of many such charters as existent there,
but adds that few of the monks can read them, or distinguish the genuine ones from the false, "of which
there are not a few". Sir Thomas regarded all his
three vellum charters with suspicion.

But it seems far more likely that Simonides had

come by these documents more or less as he declared than that he had forged them himself.

It does not appear that Simonides attempted to sell any other manuscripts of his collection whilst he was in England between 1853 and 1855. His manuscripts he declared amounted at that time to 2,500, and to have forged them all he must, as he said, have lived longer than Methusaleh. At a later date he had chests full of MSS. in London, of which Mr. C. Stewart, his biographer, declared that, had he possessed a factory, he could not have manufactured them in a lifetime. What became of them all after Simonides had died of leprosy at Alexandria in 1867 it is impossible now to ascertain.

But the temptation to deceive was born of its seducing facility, and Simonides was no votary of strict veracity. From December, 1854, till April, 1855, he was in Paris, and whilst there became acquainted with the Count de Marcellus, who was collecting materials for a work on Nonnus, the Greek poet of the fifth century who wrote the *Dionysiacs* and versified the Gospel of St. John. Could Simonides throw any light on Nonnus? Simonides thought so, and after a fortnight came a fairly full account of Nonnus from the lost work of Demetrius Magnes, *On Poets and Writers of the same Names*, a work referred to by name and ascribed to Demetrius by Diogenes Laertius (i., 112; v., 3).

But Demetrius Magnes wrote this work in the time of Cicero, and can therefore have hardly testified to Nonnus, who lived six centuries later! Simonides seems to have overlooked this fact, and to have identified Demetrius Magnes with a Dionysius, a Libyan archbishop (according to him) of the sixth century, to whom he attributed the work *On Poets and Writers of the same Names*, which had been written many centuries earlier. This mistake vitiated all the information he drew from this source. It was from this same work of Demetrius Magnes, in the first century B.C., that he sketched the life of his famous Uranius, the Alexandrian writer of the fourth century A.D. as well as of Hermas, and of Horus, the Egyptian.

The Count de Marcellus testifies to the sedentary and industrious life led by Simonides in Paris; he describes him as taciturn, gloomy and suspicious, and as dressed always in black. He testifies also to his indifference to gain, and expresses his belief that during the whole time he was in France he made no attempt to sell any of his MSS. (*Athenæum Français*, 23rd February, 1856).

The Shepherd of Hermas.

But it was otherwise in Germany, whither he went in July, 1855. His sojourn in Leipsic is famous for his dealings with two works, of which one was the first known Greek copy of the *Shepherd of Hermas*. The first three leaves of this had been extracted by him from a copy still existing in the monastery of St. Gregory on Mount Athos; six other leaves were a copy of a remaining portion left at Mount Athos. It was for long disputed to what extent this copied portion, and another copy by Simonides, corresponded with the original, but the recent discovery of the remainder of the original at St. Gregory seems to absolve Simonides from the charge of any worse crime than an endeavour to emendate a very mutilated text, and to help himself by translating the conclusion from the Latin translation. Professor Dindorf bought this Hermas for the very moderate price of 100 thalers, and there it is in the University Library at Leipsic to this day.

But in the Imperial Library at Vienna there is another bit of Simonides' work, namely, a portion of a palimpsest of the same Hermas, which was included in the original negotiation with Dindorf, but restored to Simonides after the discovery of the Uranius fraud. It is entered in May, 1856, as follows: " Two leaves of an alleged Greek palimpsest parchment : a gift of Simonides, a proof of the art of fabrication of the same learned man, being received and given as such " (Hilgenfeld's *Hermas*, 1887, Int. xii.). This must mean that it was presented to the library as a specimen of the author's skill in calligraphy, though Simonides always spoke of it as one of the most valuable works in the possession of the library.

The Egyptian History of Uranius.

The other work which Simonides tried to dispose of at Leipsic was the celebrated Uranius. But this palimpsest Simonides never admitted to be a forgery, and at a later date he is said to have refused good offers for it from Sir T. Phillipps and the library at Vienna. In any case the story in connexion with it can never fail to edify and amuse mankind.

To a young fellow-countryman studying theology at Leipsic Simonides had from time to time sent from London certain Greek documents to correct; strange as it may seem that Simonides at the age of thirty-five should have needed such aid from a youth who was still a mere student. With this student, Alexander Lycurgus, in later times an archbishop in the Greek Church, Simonides lived in 1855 in the same house at Leipsic for three months. Lycurgus, who did not know what a palimpsest was, and was quite ignorant of palæography, was led to suspect that his friend was forging a palimpsest, and when Simonides offered the Hermas and Uranius to Professor Dindorf, Lycurgus thought it his duty to warn Dindorf of his suspicions. Dindorf replied that to deceive Dindorf was a very different thing from deceiving the English, and that chemical tests would soon detect forgery. The test being applied, the very faded underlying letters came out blue, as they had to do if genuinely old, which convinced Dindorf that Lycurgus' warnings were the offspring of jealousy. The letters, moreover, were real Greek letters, and when Lycurgus pointed out that the phrase κατ' ἐμὴν ἰδέαν ("in my opinion") savoured of modern rather than of ancient usage the great German scholar pronounced the phrase quite unexceptionable (" Er fand in dieser Phrase alles griechisch," Lycurgus' *Enthüllangen*).

Dindorf's share in the transaction was as little satisfactory from the financial as it was from the classical point of view. Towards the end of November, 1855, he agreed to give Simonides 2,000 thalers for his Uranius, and on 1st January, 1856, before starting to Berlin with the Uranius, he declared his intention of asking 5,000 thalers for it from the Prussian Government. The genuineness of Uranius commending itself to Lepsius and to most of the Academy at Berlin, the King of Prussia was induced to offer this sum for the work; nor would Dindorf leave it at Berlin before Lepsius had advanced 2,500 thalers in part payment for it. On 15th January Simonides duly received his 2,000 thalers from Dindorf, but before Dindorf had gone to Berlin, Simonides had offered to refund the 2,000 thalers if he had any doubt of the genuineness of the document. Before the king had paid the stipulated sum, events occurred which cut short the transaction; but had nothing intervened, it would appear that whilst Simonides would have stood to gain 2,000 thalers from Uranius, Dindorf would have stood to gain 3,000.

And so convinced was he of the value of Uranius that he arranged to get it published at Oxford, and wrote for it a Latin preface which duly came out at Oxford under the title of *Uranii Alexandrini de Regibus Egyptorum Libri tres*, but, on the very day that it appeared, came news from Berlin that the whole thing was considered a fraud, so that not more than fifteen copies of this wonderful preface with ten pages of specimens of the Greek text came into circulation. The month of January had not passed before Lepsius at Berlin and Tischendorf at Leipsic had come to the conclusion that the Uranius was a forgery. Chemical tests and the microscope are said to have lent support to the historical doubts of Lepsius and to the palæographical objections of Tischendorf. Then arose a fierce dispute between Leipsic and Berlin as to which had first been so clever as to detect the fraud. But for Simonides the important thing was that Lepsius came to Leipsic with the Director of Police, and had him arrested, and conveyed to Berlin to take his trial. There by good fortune, the Berlin magistracy, disclaiming jurisdiction, acquitted him, and let him go free.

Among the things which Lepsius says were found in the Greek's possession at the time of his arrest were a number of false and *genuine* MSS.; the original Greek copy of Uranius; rusty nails for the production of yellow ink; and books, including those of Lepsius and Bunsen; and the untouched 2,000 thalers from Dindorf.

But Simonides contended that he had only used coloured ink for making clearer the almost illegible letters of the original text; as for the rusty nails, he had from his youth been accustomed to drink water impregnated with iron, and he used these nails to turn common water into iron water! This would hardly find credence with a British jury, but as Dindorf had insisted on getting a Greek transcript of Uranius, the supposed original copy was probably the transcript, and produced after and not before the palimpsest.

But the strangest thing concerns the books of Lepsius. This scholar, the leading Egyptologist of his day, had written books containing his ideas of the proper order of the Egyptian kings; nor would anything have been easier for Simonides than to have constructed his Uranian history in accordance with Lepsius' conclusions. Lycurgus in fact charged him with having done so, and accounted in that way for Lepsius' readiness at first to accept Uranius as genuine. But from Lepsius' own account it is quite clear that what made him first suspect the Uranius was its divergence from his own historical preconceptions. Judging *a priori*, this divergence was exactly what one would not have expected in a forgery. For what object could a forger have in making his list of kings conflict with all previous lists? Take, for instance, the first dynasty (so-called) beginning with Menes, and including eight names in Manetho's list; why should Simonides have to some extent altered the names and increased the number of these kings? Why have given names to 138 kings before Menes when a total historical blank in those days covered the time before Menes; and why in nearly every detail have gone out of his way to clash with the received Egyptology of his day?

Such a course was bound to prove fatal to Uranius on the most cursory inspection by a competent scholar.

But it is remarkable that whilst Lepsius did thus condemn the Uranius on historical grounds, he did not accept Tischendorf's palæographical objections to it. He considered the uncial writing of the underlying text to be written in a masterly style in the manner of the first century of our era. A newspaper quarrel between him and Tischendorf ensued on this point, and even after the arrest of Simonides Lepsius continued to question Tischendorf on the grounds of his objections, feeling evidently some misgiving about them.

Tischendorf was only the senior of Simonides by five years, and in the science of palæography had neither his knowledge nor his experience. He based his claim to a decision on the ground of a close acquaintance with nearly fifty palimpsests and more than 120 Greek uncial MSS. His judgment was correct with regard to the Hermas palimpsest, but admittedly the two palimpsests had the appearance of a wide difference in age, and it may be doubted whether his condemnation of the Uranius was not as much prompted by an antecedent disbelief in anything Simonidean as by such real palæographical tests as the subsequent advance of palæography would now deem conclusive. It does not appear that any palæographical objections came from the Academy of Berlin. Tischendorf had the glory of these to himself, and they failed to convince a scholar like Lepsius.

The really fatal flaw in Uranius was the ascription of a life of him to Dionysius or Demetrius Magnes. For how in a work written in the time of Cicero could there have been any mention of a writer living some centuries later? But this difficulty seems never to have occurred to the learned men of Leipsic and Berlin.

Simonides after all his troubles, being banished from Saxony, betook himself straight to Vienna, and in the autumn of the same year published a vigorous defence of himself and his Uranius at Munich (*Archæologische Abhandlungen*). To this he was compelled by the obstinate refusal of the Augsburg *Allgemeine Zeitung* to print the letters he wrote in explanation of his conduct. This was the more regrettable in that the same paper had published on 29th November, 1853, a most damaging account of Simonides' antecedents at Athens and Constantinople by Dr. Mordtman, an account which was reproduced by the *Athenæum* on 23rd February, 1856. It is impossible to verify Dr. Mordtman's stories, and political partisanship ran so high at the time that only a qualified credence can be attached to them. But assuming Simonides to have been guilty of the rascalities ascribed to him, how was it that they in no way affected his friendship with the immaculate Lycurgus, with whom he constantly corresponded and in whose house he also

4 *

resided for three months in 1855? Lycurgus acted
as interpreter between Dindorf and Simonides; why
did he not warn Dindorf from the first, if he believed
these stories, that he was dealing with a convicted
swindler? The line of high moral superiority taken
by Lycurgus is by no means justified by his own
account of his relations with Simonides.

That there really existed a writer called Uranius
is proved by the frequent allusions to him by
Stephanus of Byzantium, the Greek grammarian of
the fifth or sixth century. But Simonides' claim for
him that he composed as many as sixty works, in-
clusive of the three books on the kings of Egypt,
rests only on the authority of Demetrius or Dionysius Magnes in his aforesaid work *On Poets
and Writers of the same Names*, written some
centuries before the supposed age of Uranius.
Simonides seems to have spoken as if all these
works were in his possession : works dealing with
the customs and dwellings of the Egyptians, with the
archæology and the kings of Ethiopia, with Arabian
history, with Lybia, Lycia, Caria and so forth. Is
it possible that he possessed or contemplated forging
palimpsests dealing with all these subjects? It can
only be replied that, having regard to the works
actually published by Simonides and to the list of
those which he wrote but did not publish, quoted in
the *Memoir* of him by his friend Charles Stewart,
nothing was impossible to the extraordinary industry
and versatility of this wonderful being.

His travels corresponded with his literary activity. After the Uranius episode he seems to have travelled widely in Europe, visiting all the chief libraries, and returning to London in April, 1858. In 1857 he edited or rather wrote three numbers of a magazine in Greek and German called *Memnon*. It is mainly devoted to an exposition of the author's theories about Egyptian hieroglyphics, and is prefaced by an introduction which reads like a showman's opening of a circus. It gives the names of 112 lost Egyptian writers, and many other wonders. It also contains a defence of Uranius and a comparison of several alleged copies of the *Shepherd of Hermas*.

THE MAYER PAPYRI.

But it was not till 1860 that Simonides again came prominently before the world. When he did so, he as usual caused a stir.

It was on 13th February that he called on Mr. Joseph Mayer of Liverpool with a request to inspect his celebrated museum of antiquities.

On 22nd February he dedicated to Mr. Mayer, "as a small mark of his personal attachment," his *Brief Dissertation on Hieroglyphic Letters*, in explanation of five Egyptian antiquities in the Museum. It was published in Greek and English by Mr. David Nutt, abounds with ingenious interpretations of the hieroglyphic characters, and frequently quotes the authority of Uranius.

But the great discovery was to follow. Mr.

Mayer had acquired, partly by purchase from a dealer called Sams and partly from the Rev. H. Stobart, a number of papyri which he had never examined and which had remained in a state of neglect. The difficult work of unrolling these papyri, of fixing them on canvas, and of deciphering them, was conducted by Simonides in the Museum, in the presence, more or less constant, of Mr. Mayer himself, of the Curator of the Museum, and of Mr. John Eliot Hodgkin. It was. not till August that some of these papyri were removed to Simonides' own house for purposes of further examination. The discovery therefore on 1st May of certain fragments of St. Matthew's Gospel on one of these papyri would seem to have been made under conditions which rendered fraud impossible or unlikely. Yet the information appended at the end to the effect that the Gospel had been written at the dictation of St. Matthew by Nicolaus the Deacon in the fifteenth year after the Ascension savoured of the highest improbability. And if the papyrus was genuine, it was the oldest known Christian document in existence.

No wonder the literary world was excited. And the excitement grew as the finds grew in number. Within a few months Simonides had discovered fragments from the Epistles of St. James and of St. Jude ; portions of eight chapters of the Book of Genesis ; the Ten Commandments ; the *Periplus* of Hanno ; the first page of a work by Aristæus ; some fragments of Zoroaster ; seven epistles of Hermippus ; and a fragment of Androsthenes, an admiral of Alexander the Great.

In this case there was no question of making profit out of MSS., forged or genuine ; the MSS. were the property of Mr. Mayer, and Simonides' only concern with them was their decipherment. But the name of Simonides excited suspicion, though the motive as well as the opportunity of forgery were not discernible.

The Mayer papyri were exhibited and examined at a meeting of the Royal Society of Literature on the evenings of 9th and 10th January, 1863, Sir F. Madden, Sir H. Rawlinson, Simonides and others being present. The Report of the Council was read on 11th February, and was strongly condemnatory of the genuineness of the documents. The condemnation was founded on such facts as the similarity in the handwriting of the MSS., albeit they purported to be of different ages ; the juxtaposition of different dates and characters on the same papyrus ; the unusual length of the lines of the writing ; the difference in the colour of most of the papyri from that of genuine papyri. And one papyrus was denounced as "a rank forgery" by reason of certain little flecks of red blotting-paper which Mr. C. W. Goodwin discovered, and which he maintained had been used to erase the Hieratic writing in order to make place for the subsequent Greek writing. But it is questionable whether this blotting-paper had

not been legitimately used in the difficult work of
unrolling and mounting the papyri previous to deciphering them.   And the admission that Simonides
exhibited two rolls of Hieratic writing, "the genuineness of which was not doubtful," sets one wondering
whether the conclusions of the majority of the Council
were correct, or would stand the test of the great
advance that has since been made in the science of
palæography.

Simonides published excellent facsimiles in 1861
and 1864 of most of these papyri.   But it is best to
inspect the originals as he mounted them himself in
the Museum of the Free Public Library at Liverpool,
where they may still be seen, together with tracings
taken by him for his lithographed facsimiles.   It is
almost impossible to believe in his manufacture of
these papyri.   They correspond in writing and appearance with numberless other papyri which have
of recent years been discovered and published.   And
there are in the collection three papyri, still unrolled,
time-worn and brittle, looking like huge cigars, and
containing no one knows what precious secrets of
antiquity.   If these are forgeries, they can hardly
be forgeries by Simonides; and if he was guiltless
in respect of these, he was presumably guiltless in
respect of the others.

One of the chief objections urged in 1863 against
these papyri was the similarity of the handwriting
in documents belonging to widely different periods.
But this similarity is the last thing that can be fairly

predicated of them. Let any one compare the two
volumes of the facsimiles, and it is rather the
diversity than the similarity of the handwriting
which will strike his attention.

As little force can now be attached to another
argument urged at the time against the papyri by
Mr. Vaux, secretary to the Literary Society, in an
Athenæum review of Simonides' facsimiles (7th
December, 1861). Mr. Vaux laid it down dog-
matically as "an undoubted fact that no MSS. of
any kind, if we except the Hieratic papyri, are known
to ascend to the first or second century, and that of
those of the fourth or fifth there are not more than
five or six throughout all the libraries of Europe".
Therefore, it was argued, these papyri, for many of
which Simonides claimed the first century, could not
be genuine. But since recent discoveries in Egypt
have carried many Greek papyri manuscripts as far
back even as the third and fourth century B.C., this
argument has ceased to exist.

In short, if these Mayer papyri are to continue
to be regarded as spurious, it ought to be only after
an impartial re-study of them, and a clear statement
of the palæographical reasons for differentiating them
from others which are accepted as genuine.

In a manuscript letter of Charles Stewart, who
wrote the *Memoir of Simonides*, the following interesting description gives a vivid picture of the
man as he appeared at that time in England: "He
was," says Stewart, "one of the most remarkable-

looking men I have ever seen.   Rather under the
middle stature he appeared bodily to be nothing
but bones and muscles, but it was not his body but
his head that was remarkable.   Immense black
whiskers, moustache, and imperial; huge black
eyebrows; an enormous mass of jet-black glossy
and curly hair, parted very much on one side and
all thrown over on to the other; deep-sunk but fiery
and piercing eyes; dark swarthy visage; massive lips
and strongly marked mouth made up a face not
easily forgotten.   But the forehead is in itself a
marvel.   For about the height of an ordinary forehead it rises perpendicularly and is exactly what a
phrenologist would call a finely developed organisa-
tion, but above this rises a second forehead, only the
second storey takes its rise one step farther back
than the first.   This step forms a kind of ledge.   The
consequence is that when he puts his hat on it only
covers the top forehead, and as that recedes a long
way back the outside rim of the hat is level with
the bridge of the nose.   The effect is curious in the
extreme with the proprietor of this double-storied
forehead."

But Stewart's *Memoir* of his Greek friend cannot
be wholly trusted.   For Stewart of course could only
impart what Simonides chose to tell him, and what
Simonides told was not necessarily the truth.
Simonides, for instance, always said that his father
had died in early life, leaving him to the care of his
uncle Benedict, head of the monastery of Pantelemon

or Russico on Mount Athos. But Simonides left in England a number of letters from his father to himself, which I have seen, and one of these is dated as late as 1862.

THE SINAITIC CODEX.

This fact of course throws doubt on all that rests only on the word of Simonides. But it does not absolutely disprove all his assertions, of which by far the most amazing was his claim to have written when at Mount Athos in 1840 the Sinaitic Codex (Codex A), which Tischendorf discovered at Mount Sinai under highly singular circumstances between the years 1844 and 1859. The claim of Simonides to have transcribed this Codex, at the suggestion of his alleged uncle Benedict, as an intended present for the Czar Nicholas I., was first publicly made in the *Guardian* of 5th September, 1862, and in the *Literary Churchman* on 16th December of the same year. Nor could anything be more precise and circumstantial in detail, or more temperate in tone than the letters in which this claim was made. The implication that Tischendorf had mistaken a manuscript of the nineteenth century for one of the fourth naturally roused that irascible theologian to a condition of fury.

That Simonides was a good enough calligrapher, even at an early age, to have written the Codex, is hardly open to doubt, and it is in his favour that the world was first indebted to him in 1856 for the

opening chapters in Greek of the *Shepherd of
Hermas*, with a portion of which the Codex Sinaiticus
actually terminates.   The coincidence seems almost
more singular than can be accounted for by chance.

But the experts in palæography were strongly
on the side of Tischendorf.   Tregelles, the distinguished scholar and Plymouth Brother, declared that
a man might as well pretend that the Alexandrian
or the Vatican MS. was a modern work as claim
to have written the Sinaitic Codex.   And the famous
Mr. Henry Bradshaw, who with Tregelles had inspected the Codex itself at Tischendorf's house at
Leipsic in July, 1862, declared himself, in a letter to
the *Guardian* of 23rd January, 1863, as being "as
absolutely certain of the genuineness and antiquity
of the Codex Sinaiticus as of his own existence".
And Mr. Scrivener, who made the Sinaitic Codex
his special study, expressed himself equally strongly
against the claim of Simonides.

Nevertheless these dogmatic assurances are not
quite convincing.   Simonides' claim was supported
on its first appearance by certain letters in the
Guardian purporting to come from Alexandria and
signed "Kallinikos Hieromonachos".   These letters,
inspected at a meeting of the Society of Literature,
were thought to be in a handwriting identical with
that of Simonides and to be written on paper like
that used in Simonides' own letters; the inference
being that Simonides had written them himself and
sent them to Alexandria to be posted back to Eng-

land (*Parthenon*, 14th February, 1863). But this alleged similarity of handwriting was never certified by any expert in handwriting.

And the attempt to throw doubt on the existence of Kallinikos failed as completely as the attempt to dispose in the same way of Benedict. Other Greeks besides Simonides had lax ideas of the value of truth. There was Nicolaides, who had been Archdeacon of Salonica from 1839 to 1853; who had visited Mount Athos five times; and who claimed to know all the MSS. existing there intimately; he wrote to the *Parthenon* that he not only had never heard of Benedict but that he disbelieved in his existence. Yet one has only to refer to Lampros' Catalogue of the Mount Athos MSS. to find Benedict's name appended to several MSS., and to one as late as 1844 (though Simonides gave 1840 as the year of his death). (See Nos. 5999, 6118, 6194, 6360, 6362, 6393.) The same work attests as conclusively the real existence of Kallinikos. A MS. dated March, 1867, is signed with the hand of Kallinikos who is "also the least of the monks of the monastery of Russico" (*i.e.*, Pantelemon) (No. 638). And there is another MS. at Pantelemon, copied by the hand of Constantine Simonides on 27th March, 1841 (6405), and two other copies of the same work by Kallinikos Monachos (6406, 6407), which prove that Kallinikos and Simonides were at Pantelemon at the same time and associated in the same work.

Simonides, who was always most precise in his
information about real or feigned persons, declares
that this Kallinikos was born in 1802, a Thessalian,
named originally Kuriakos; on his admission to the
Church he took the name of Kallinikos, and for his
bravery in the war of the Greek Revolution he
received the surname of Keraunos. Whether this
was so or not, Kallinikos was a real person, and his
intervention in the controversy with his attestation of
having seen Simonides write the Codex cannot be
brushed aside as the testimony of a fabulous being.

In fact it is upon Kallinikos that the whole
question hinges. For Kallinikos is said to have had
lithographed at Moscow in 1853 and at Odessa in
1854 certain letters between himself and Simonides
and the patriarch Constantius, wherein repeated allusion is made to the Codex prepared by Simonides
for the Czar. One of these collections of lithographed letters is called "Autographa" and the other
"Spoudaion hupomnema". They are both at the
British Museum, presented apparently by Mr. James
Young, the eminent antiquary, who received them
as a gift from Simonides. But were these letters
really lithographed in the years assigned to them
in the frontispiece? May they not have been concocted by Simonides in 1863 and then antedated
by ten years in order to support his claim? This
has never been satisfactorily settled. Mr. John
Eliot Hodgkin set himself the task in 1863 of trying
to arrive at the truth, and he was informed by a

"correspondent of unquestionable reputation at Odessa" that the foreman of certain lithographing works in that city perfectly remembered the printing of the letters at the time alleged. But in the case of Simonides, who was well skilled in lithography, one would be glad of some stronger proof.

As such proof Simonides showed Mr. Hodgkin a letter to himself at Munich from a friend B. Panchalos in London, dated March, 1858, which refers chiefly to these publications by Kallinikos in 1853. A copy of this letter in the handwriting of Simonides is still in the possession of Mr. Hodgkin, with a note by him, to the effect that the original letter was in a peculiar writing and that the post-marks seemed to be real ones. The writer professes to have brought from Odessa to London the letters and some works by Simonides which Kallinikos had lithographed. But Mr. Hodgkin's note bears the date of 21st July, 1863, and it is conceivable that the original letter had been produced at a later date than its apparent one.

But if these lithographed letters really were produced in the fifties, long before Simonides made his claim, and if they prove the truth of his statements concerning his work on the Codex, it is of course possible to maintain that it was not the Sinaitic Codex which he produced, but another. Simonides claimed to have seen his own work, the Codex, at Mount Sinai, when he was there in 1852, and his most important lithographed letters are dated from Mount Sinai in

the March and April of 1852.   But was Simonides at
Mount Sinai at that time ?   Stewart says, presumably
on the authority of Simonides himself, that he went to
Mount Athos for the third time in 8th October, 1851,
and that he stayed there a whole year, which of course
is wholly incompatible with his writing letters from
Mount Sinai in the March and April of 1852.   But
again Stewart may have made a mistake about the
dates, and it would be unfair to press his statement too
strongly against Simonides.

It is to be regretted that this matter was never
cleared up at the time the claim was made.   It cannot
be said to have been settled by the mere opinions of
Tregelles or Bradshaw, or by the more critical and
palæographical objections urged by Mr. Scrivener in
his *Introduction to the Sinaitic Codex* (1867).   The
two former examined the Codex two months before
Simonides had made his claim to it as his work, so
that they had no reason to examine it with suspicion.
And Mr. Scrivener's argument that no mere youth of
at most nineteen could in a few months have composed a volume of nearly 4,000,000 uncial letters,
though convincing about most youths, is not convincing where that youth was Simonides.   On the
side of Simonides is his unlimited skill in calligraphy ;
the very audacity of such a claim if entirely baseless ;
the remarkable presence in the Codex of a portion of
the *Shepherd of Hermas*, which Simonides was the
first scholar ever to have seen in Greek ; the very
natural allusions to the work in the lithographed

letters; the fact that no visitor to the monastery at Mount Sinai before 1844 had ever seen or heard of such a work as belonging to the monks; and the very extraordinary story told by Tischendorf of his discovery and acquisition of the Codex. The question therefore, pending the acquisition of further evidence, must remain among the interesting but unsolved mysteries of literature.

Simonides appears to have left England somewhat hurriedly in 1864, nor is it known what became of him between that date and the year 1867 when he died, or at least is said to have died, at Alexandria (*Notes and Queries* for 22nd October, 1867, 3rd Series, xii., 339). His literary activity was extraordinary. Besides the works he published in Odessa, in England and in Germany, he wrote many others which were never published. His chief interest was to prove that his method of interpreting Egyptian hieroglyphics was superior to as well as different from that of Champollion and other Egyptologists, and it may be suspected that he was often not above resorting to trickery in support of his theory. His learning was prodigious, but it occasionally failed him, as where he placed the death of Irenæus in 292 (a full century after the probable or possible date), and where he drew on Demetrius Magnes for information which that writer could by no possibility have supplied. It was from Demetrius (or Dionysius) Magnes that he drew, as from an inexhaustible well, for his extraordinarily minute information about numberless

5

people, many of whom were long posterior in date to their alleged biographer. But Simonides did not always invent or forge or lie; probably these lapses occupied the smaller portion of his activity, and much of his work was honest, laborious and useful. But naturally discrimination in these circumstances was difficult or impossible, and his contemporaries found it the easier course to reject as spurious anything connected with his name. It is probable that scepticism has gone farther than was necessary in this direction, and that literature has lost in consequence some acquisitions that rightfully belong to it. But of all the figures of the nineteenth century that are connected with the shady side of literature, Simonides, with his extensive learning, his knowledge of manuscripts, his miraculous calligraphy, his passionate nature, and above all his claim to the authorship of the Sinaitic Codex, will ever stand out as pre-eminently the first of his order. In literary ability he surpassed all his contemporaries, but unhappily the essential element of truth formed no part of his mental constitution.

CHAPTER IV.

ITALIAN FORGERY: ANNIUS OF VITERBO.

THE forged literature of the world in general or of a particular country presents the spectacle of an inexhaustible mine, the contemplation of which fills an explorer with consternation as he thinks of the marvellous ability and industry displayed in the illicit working of its glittering veins. His only course in such bewilderment is to concentrate his attention on a few particular workers, and to study the writings of those who in this line of labour have attained to most distinction and made their names in some sense representative of the nationalities that produced them.

Of all the forgeries, detected or undetected, in the Italian world of letters, none is more famous than that associated with the name of Annius (whose real name was Nannius) of Viterbo, who lived from 1432 to 1502, when he is said to have been poisoned for his too unreserved denunciations of the infamies of Cæsar Borgia. It is certain that Annius contributed more to the confusion of literature, whether innocently or not, than any man of his own or of any other generation.

And it was perhaps therefore fitting that in the year 1558 his painted figure should have been placed on one of the walls of the municipal palace at the place on which his learning cast a sort of lustre.

Annius belonged to the order of Preaching Brothers or Dominicans, and was a man of mark in his generation. In 1471, when in his fortieth year, he preached certain sermons at Genoa which subsequently were published as his first book under the title of *Tractatus de Imperio Turcarum*, or a treatise on the rule of the Turk, a subject of very lively interest in Europe, when twenty years had not yet passed since the capture of Constantinople by the Turk. This first work was followed nine years later (1480) by the publication of some more sermons, based on the Book of Revelations, entitled *De futuris Christianorum triumphis in Turcas et Saracenas*, wherein the preacher foretold an earlier termination of the Ottoman Empire than history has yet had the happiness to see fulfilled.

The evils of lending money on interest next occupied his literary activity (1492), and in 1499, in the papacy of the notorious Alexander VI., he was raised to the position of Master of the Vatican. To this office the duty appertained of examining, correcting, rejecting, or approving everything that was printed at Rome; all libraries and printers were under his jurisdiction; and he had a right to a seat on the Congregation of the Index.

Yet the very year preceding the attainment of

this post of literary autocrat Annius had himself
published a work which generally counts among the
marvels of literary falsification! This was his famous
De Comentariis Antiquitatum, published at Rome
in 1498. He had moreover the reputation of being
half-demented, for so at least Scaliger was led to believe (Scaligerana, i., 195: "Annius Viterbensis a
été vu par un homme qui me l'a dit il etait fou et
talis habebatur").

So that his appointment to this particular post
was as incongruous as it was possible to be, in the
light of subsequent knowledge.

Annius opened his work with a fulsome dedica-
tion to Ferdinand and Isabella of Spain, and then
proceeded to a preface on the special duty of himself
as a professor of theology towards the truth and
towards his country. To defend the glory and antiquity of his country, nay, of the whole of Europe,
was his aim; and though he could lay no claim
to elegance of language, he could claim to give
the "sole and simple truth". He would yield to
others the point of language, but not that of the
discovery of truth. If any critics objected, let them
come forward in his lifetime, when he would forthwith answer them; let them not wait till he was
dead.

The work consisted of seventeen distinct treatises,
of which eleven were by different writers, who had
been lost to the world till their discovery by Annius.
The texts of these authors he interspersed with the

most prolix commentaries of his own, these constituting by far the larger part of his voluminous
work.   And if genuine the authors themselves
were well deserving of comment, for they would
have thrown light on some of the remotest and
darkest periods of history.   Priceless would they
have been, had their authenticity only been above
suspicion.

It is impossible to do more than glance at the
several lost works of ancient times which Annius
claimed to have recovered for the world.

1. That Myrsilus, a Lesbian of unknown date,
wrote an account of the origins of Italy and Etruria
is known by the references made to him by ancient
writers, and notably by Dionysius of Halicarnassus,
who, treating of the same obscure and vexed question
of the origin of Etruria, borrowed much from him
for the first book of his *Antiquities.*   Annius says
with truth that a reader of Dionysius might seem to
be reading Myrsilus, as given by himself.   But
Annius, or another, might have produced Myrsilus
by the help of Dionysius.

Nothing could be more ingenious than his account
of the colonisation of Italy by the misty Pelasgian
and other tribes of Greek origin, and his treatment
of the question of the Lydian or of the aboriginal
beginnings of Etruria.   But the authenticity of
Myrsilus admits unfortunately of more dispute.

2. About his discovery of twenty-two fragments
of Cato the Censor, who was known to have written

a work on the origins of Italy, Annius vouchsafes information, which he subsequently applies to nine of
his discoveries. He tells us that he found his Cato
in the ancient collections of a certain Master William
of Mantua. Cato had been stirred to write of the
splendid origin of Italy in the Golden Age by the
impudent claim of the Greeks to have been the first
colonisers of Italy. The work breathes just the anti-
Greek spirit one would expect to find in Cato the
Censor, and abounds in complaints of Greek mendacity, Greek vanity and Greek verbosity.

The information is mostly geographical, dealing
with the origins of Italian towns and people, as Pliny
also dealt with them in the third book of his *Natural
History*. Pliny refers to Cato's work, and probably
borrowed from it. But may not these fragments of
Cato, belonging to Master William of Mantua, have
been borrowed from Pliny and other writers? A
certain passage in Pliny closely resembles Cato in the
names of Etrurian towns, but the order of the names
is different, as one would expect, if Pliny had been
the mine from which these fragments of Cato had
been hewn. But the fragments cannot have been
an easy work to compile, and the learning of their
accompanying commentaries is prodigious.

3. Caius Sempronius, we know from Dionysius
of Halicarnassus, busied himself, like Cato, with the
origins of the Italian cities. Annius professes to have
failed to find this work, but suggests that one he
found and commented on, *De Divisione et Choro-*

graphia Italiæ, was the same.   Much is therein told
of the geography of the Alps and of the towns of
Italy, and we learn that Rome did not derive its
name from Romulus, having been founded by Saturn
in the Golden Age many centuries earlier.   This
Sempronian work resembles that of Cato very much
both in its substance and in its style.   Sempronius
also condemns the levity, mendacity and boastfulness
of the writers of Greece ; but this anti-Greek animus
appears also in Annius himself, constituting a strong
and suspicious family likeness between all the three
writers.

4. Quintus Fabius Pictor was one of the oldest
and best historians of Rome, who lived and took
actual part in the Gallic war (B.C. 225) and in the
second Punic war.   His history has not come down
to us, but Annius found two books of his, treating
respectively of the Golden Age and of the topography
of the hills of Rome.   Pretty is his description of
that Age, which lasted till the reign of Ninus, King
of Assyria, and so like that of Ovid that one would
think the poet had borrowed from Pictor or Pictor
from the poet.   And indeed Pictor describes the
original ground of Rome as " a pasture for oxen "
(*pascua bobus erat*), Cato also strangely enough using
the same identical words ; but the words are borrowed
from Ovid who says of early Rome :—

" Tantaque res paucis *pascua bobus erat* " (*Fasti*, i.,
244).   How came Cato and Pictor to quote Ovid
more than a century before Ovid was born ?

5. Archilochus was a Greek chronographer who flourished, Annius thinks, about the twenty-ninth Olympiad, that is, about the year 664. In the few pages which Annius recovered from Archilochus' work on dates (*De Temporibus*) we find Archilochus in agreement with Pictor about the Golden Age that preceded Ninus; and he tells us of five kings of Troy before Priam and of seven distinct Homers who lived before the famous poet, twenty-four years before his own time. Archilochus, a shadowy figure himself, derives his chronology from one more shadowy still, from Maseas Phenix Damascenus, who belongs to the absolutely impenetrable mist.

6. Metasthenes, an historian of the Persian annals, was another chronographer of whom Annius was so fortunate as to find a Latin translation. He was a Persian priest, and to be distinguished from Megasthenes, a Greek historian, who was no priest at all. It is singular that Metasthenes should begin with an allusion to the credibility of priests in general, and particularly of that other priest of Babylon, Berosus, five of whose lost books Annius also had the happiness to discover. And he proceeds to give an analysis of the reigns of the Assyrian kings, as given by Berosus; and so he continues with his list of dates down to the time of Alexander the Great.

7. Another work of a similar chronological nature introduced to the world by Annius was the *Breviarium*

de Temporibus by Philo Judæus. It was so called as being a "brief" summary of historical time from Adam down to his own time. Other works by Philo have been discovered since the days of Annius, some of which are accounted genuine and others spurious. Annius expresses his wonder that this *Breviarium* had come to be so neglected of theologians and bishops, since it contained so much good material against the Jews ; but how could they have neglected what was non-existent? And it is remarkable how similar in style is this dull chronology of Jewish history to the preceding chronologies of Archilochus and Metasthenes.

8. Annius could not discover who Xenophon (not the historian) was, but he thought that he was the son of Griphon and lived about the year 400. At all events Annius became possessed of a Latin translation of his treatise *De Equivocis*, about different people or things bearing similar names. He could tell us of the several bearers of the name of Homer, of Ninus, of Ogyges, or of Cadmus, also of the several floods that have left a tradition in history. And his information is conveyed in the same terse and simple manner which characterises all these lost writers, and is confirmative of their statements on many points.

9. Two fragments of an *Itinerary* of Antoninus Pius are not the least curious documents in this medley collection. These are expressly referred to the collection of Master William, made in the year

1315. It was the piety of Antonine, according to Annius, which caused him to produce this *Itinerary* of the whole world; it was to make travelling easier for the poor, for strangers, for fugitives, or for soldiers. And as it was for the use of people of all nationalities, and it was only the Italians who measured distances by miles, it gave the names of towns in their order but not the distances between them. In this respect it differed from other Itineraries claiming to be that of Antonine; as it also did in recording six routes unrecorded elsewhere, including one by sea, leading from Rome to Gaul, with the names of the several towns passed on the way; just the names, and nothing more.

10. But the most interesting and longest of Annius' discoveries purported to be five complete books of the lost *History* of Berosus, of whose writings only sundry fragments had sailed safely down the stream of time. Berosus of Babylon lived in the third century B.C., and wrote a Greek history of Babylonia, of which modern learning has tended to confirm the accuracy; but the Berosus of Annius is another matter. He begins with the Caldæan ideas of the world before the flood; of the terrible and wicked giants; and of Noah; and of the colonisation of the world. Then he leads us through a maze of Babylonian kings, and of their contemporary kings in other parts of the world, and we wonder at Anameon, founder of Mæonia, whose reign of 150

years robs our own Parr and Henry Jenkins of their honours of longevity.

It was in the reign of Jupiter Belus, the second King of Babylon, that Tyras founded Tyre, and in the reign of Ninus, the next king, that Iberus ruled and gave his name to the Iberi. Much are we told of the inventions and travels and exploits of Osiris, and a host of mythical persons and places are treated with the honours of history in these marvellous five books of Berosus.

But how came Annius by these books of Berosus? He alludes incidentally to a monk of the name of Mathias, provincial of the Armenian Dominican Order, whom he had once entertained at Genoa, and to another Armenian in his company, a Master Georgius, from whom he received this Berosus as a gift ("a cujus socio magistro Georgio similiter Armeno hanc Berosi deflorationem dono habui").

No one can now dispute the existence of this Armenian, but it is singular that Annius should have been so fortunate as to acquire from a Master William of Mantua and a Master Georgius of Armenia these treasures of antiquity, both treating of similar topics in so similar a way.

11. Berosus, the Babylonian historian, is naturally followed by Manetho, the Egyptian. Recent Egyptian research has conferred on the fragments of Manetho's chronology of Egypt more credit than it formerly possessed, but Annius begins his history by Manetho with a king Egyptus, whose tomb as

yet has responded to no search. Contemporaries with Egyptus were Romus, King of the Celts, Faunus Priscus, King of the Aborigines, Pandion, King of Athens, and Belochus the younger, King of Assyria. And so the weary tale continues through many kings and countries, supplemented with abundant learning from Annius' inexhaustible store of mythological learning. But one thing seems fatal to his Manetho. For one certain fact about Manetho seems to be that he wrote his lost Greek history of Egypt in the reign of Ptolemy Philadelphus (B.C. 284-246); but Annius infers from an alleged comparison of the name of Pharaoh with the Roman name of Augustus for an emperor that Manetho lived some time *after* the establishment of the Roman Empire, instead of more than 200 years before it.

The genuineness of Annius' work was for long a subject of dispute among the learned, and many are the names of no mean reputation which ranged themselves at one time on the side of the Dominican monk. But the doubters ultimately carried the day, till at last we find the judgment of the nineteenth century expressed as follows by Tiraboschi in his *History of Italian Literature* (vi., 15): "There is no one who is moderately versed in the first elements of literature who does not laugh at the stories published and commented on by Annius".

But before this conclusion was reached many of these stories, told with such an air of assurance and learning, found their way into other books, to the

detriment of their credit and the mortification of
their authors. Poor Leandro Alberti, who in 1568
published a *Description of Italy*, is said to have died
of annoyance when he became aware of the worthlessness of some of the statements he had borrowed
from Annius. And doubtless there were many
others whom a tougher moral fibre enabled to sur-
vive a similar cause for vexation of spirit.

The question admits of less easy settlement, how
far Annius was personally responsible for the literary
imposture associated with his name. Was he the
guilty author of the fraud, or only its innocent
transmitter? The balance of opinion rather favours
the latter alternative, but the internal evidence
against Annius is decidedly strong.

It appears from a letter of Annius to his brother
Thomas, of the same order, that he published his
commentaries in compliance with his brother's request, and in this letter he alludes to having brought
back with him from Mantua to Viterbo nine of his
eleven rediscovered works; that is, all of them except
the Manetho and Berosus. He had returned with
the Most Reverend Cardinal Paul de Campo Fulgoso,
and brought back his fragments of Philo, Xenophon,
Sempronius, Fabius Pictor, Cato, Antonine, Metasthenes, Archilochus and Myrsilus. The inference
is that he obtained all of them, as he asserts of his
Cato, from the collection of William of Mantua. But
a strange family resemblance pervades all of them,
as well as the Berosus and Manetho, which were

presumably both the gift of the Armenian Georgius.
And, though the diversity of writers and topics
would seem to lie beyond the possible fabrication
of a single brain, it is remarkable how they all play
into one another's hands, and support one another's
statements; Methethenes, derived from the Mantuan,
corroborating Berosus, derived from the Armenian,
and Cato and the rest being generally in close
agreement with one another. And not only the
spirit but often the very words of the commentator
are very like those of his originals; Annius as well
as Cato and Sempronius denounce the mendacity of
the Greeks, and the expression *argumento est* ("for a
proof"), a favourite with Annius, occurs also in some
of his originals. And all these different writers
writing at different times give us information sur-
prisingly similar in kind to that of which Annius was
himself personally fond. Thus Berosus tells us that
it was from Macedon, son of Osiris, that Macedonia
received its name; and the modern name of Belgium
is made to descend from his Beligius, King of the
Celts. Manetho is responsible for Paris, another
King of the Celts, as the father of our modern
Parisians in the time of Menophis, second King of
Egypt; for Phenix, the founder of Phœnicia; and
for Lemannus, another Celtic king, whose name still
survives in the alternative but less common name
for the lake of Geneva. Cato introduces us to King
Rhetus as giving his name to the Rhetii, and
Sempronius to Ligur, the founder of Liguria.

It is this unity of spirit throughout his collection which constitutes the greatest suspicion against Annius himself. Had he obtained them all from William of Mantua, the fabrication might have been thrown back on William; but that William should have had a Metasthenes showing an intimate knowledge of the Berosus of the Armenian Georgius, and that both these works should have fallen into the hands of Annius, passes the bounds of a credible coincidence. We are thrown back on the Dominican's own brain and on his marvellous knowledge of literature as the most probable source of his collection. If there be any truth in the nebulous tradition of an old thirteenth century Catalogue of Authors in the Colbertin Library, as the possible source of the titles of his works, it is still Annius who must be held responsible for putting these shadows into substance.

It was probably the inconceivability of any man writing so immense a work for a mere pastime or even for the propagation of his own ideas that led so many learned men at the time to believe in Annius. But among those who regarded his work as fictitious were Casaubon and Antonio Augustino, Archbishop of Tarragona. It was this Antonio, author of a work on false Italian productions of other kinds, who first told the story of Annius burying an inscribed stone near Viterbo and then contriving to have it discovered by some workmen, the said stone going to prove that Viterbo had been founded by

Isis and Osiris 2,000 years before the founding of Rome.

The " Tabula Cibellaria " in the Museum at Viterbo, found in what Annius called the Ager Cibellarius, proves that material as well as literary falsification had its attraction for the clever Dominican.

CHAPTER V.

PSALMANAZAR: THE FAMOUS FORMOSAN.

A MAN whose company Dr. Johnson would seek, in preference even to that of Richardson, the novelist; whom he would often visit in his lodgings in Iron-monger Row, Old Street, or hold converse with in a neighbouring alehouse; for whose piety Johnson had such reverence that even that arch-dissentient lost in his presence the power to contradict; and of whose exemplary penitence he would often discourse towards the close of his own life in terms of the highest praise; such a man must have been in a high degree remarkable. And remarkable indeed from first to last was George Psalmanazar, still of unknown birth and origin, who made his first appearance in London early in the eighteenth century.

When Johnson knew him Psalmanazar was about eighty; a man who earned a livelihood from his work for the booksellers, but a man who enjoyed a some-what wide notoriety for the earnestness of his piety and the regularity of his devotions. This fact about him which so impressed Johnson impressed his age no less, causing him to be so highly esteemed that the very children in his neighbourhood would not

pass him without some token of respect. Such was
the reward of a life that for about fifty years had
been consistently and sincerely religious. His exemplary life ended in 1763, in about the eighty-fourth
year of his age.

 Yet this sincerity seems to have grown out of
hypocrisy, and the self-chosen name of George Psalmanazar is connected with one of the most astonishing
frauds in the history of literature. Coming to England from the Continent, under the auspices of the
Rev. W. Innes, an army chaplain, he at once interested the religious world in his favour, by claiming
to be a native of Formosa, who had been converted
from an appalling heathenism to the truths and
practices of Christianity. No one ever guessed
rightly of what country he was a native, but there
was nothing Oriental about his skin or hair. This,
however, stood very little in his way. He found an
easy introduction to Compton, Bishop of London,
whose tenure of that see had been so eventful in the
reign of James II., and on whom he palmed off the
English Catechism translated into Formosan. Not
only did bishops and the clergy receive him gladly,
but even some men of learning declared his Formosan
language to be a real one because it was so regular
and grammatical " and so different from all they knew
both with respect to words and idioms ". This interesting proselyte, who had trained himself to eat raw
flesh the better to support his character as an Oriental,
was introduced to all men of distinction in Church

and State, and we find him dining on 9th February,
1704, with Sir Hans Sloane, and eating his meat raw
in the company of two noblemen and the Prussian
ambassador. A week before at the Royal Institution
he had held a public discussion with Father Fontenay,
who had been for eighteen years a missionary in China,
and he had responded without loss of credit to the
searching questions put to him by that doubting
Father.

Psalmanazar's own story was that he had left
Formosa six years earlier, when he was nineteen.
This would have made him twenty-five at the time
of his coming to London, but he added some years
to his real age in order to make his story more
credible. For a youth of twenty he had some right
to be regarded as a marvel. He had more than a
smattering of six languages, and wrote and spoke
Latin fluently. It was in Latin that he conversed
with Archbishop Tenison, Innes acting as interpreter,
and it was in Latin that he originally wrote his *Description of Formosa*. This, like the Catechism, he
wrote at the instigation of Innes, who, having used
him successfully as a stepping-stone to his own
preferment, afterwards deserted him. The book was
a reproduction of the many marvellous things about
Formosa he had propounded in conversation, but not
of everything. Asked, for instance, about longevity
in the island, he replied that 120 was accounted a
common age, and 100 a very moderate one; his own
grandfather had lived to 117, and was then as fresh

and vigorous as a young man, owing to his habit of sucking the blood of a viper warm every morning! But this story at least was not repeated in print. There seems to have been no limit to British credulity in the early years of Queen Anne. Good people subscribed for the support of this marvellous proselyte, and the Bishop of London had him sent to study at Christ Church, Oxford, in the pious hope that he would there instruct in Formosan some future missionaries to that promising island.

An exceedingly curious book is the *Historical and Geographical Description of Formosa, an Island subject to the Emperor of Japan*, published in 1704, and dedicated to the Bishop of London. Herodotus himself could hardly have put human credulity to a more severe strain than did Psalmanazar.

The Emperor of Japan conquered Formosa in a strange manner. Under the pretext of religion, of offering sacrifices in Formosa to the God of Formosa, he sent a great army into the country. Thirty or forty soldiers were placed in large litters, drawn by two elephants, and at the windows of these litters were placed the heads of oxen or rams, which removed all suspicion from the minds of the natives. Then the soldiers jumped out, and by threatening death to the natives secured their acceptance of the yoke of Japan without bloodshed or difficulty.

The Formosans were represented as having worshipped the heavenly bodies till two philosophers appeared, who bade them turn from this worship to

that of one Supreme God. To Him they were
bidden to raise a temple, and on an altar therein
to burn the hearts of 20,000 boys under the age of
nine. The indignant Formosans pursued these philosophers into a desert, but their persecution of them
being avenged by eclipses, storms and earthquakes,
the Formosans became penitent, and accepted a
prophet, by name Psalmanazar, or "the author of
peace," so called because he was to declare a new
peace between the Deity and the Formosans. In
the book this other Psalmanazar plays the part assigned to Moses in the Old Testament, as the
mouthpiece of the Divine commands. Most striking
of these was the command that on a given annual
festival 18,000 boys under nine should have their
hearts burnt upon an altar. This festival was the
anniversary of the day on which the Deity first appeared in the tabernacle in the form of an ox, when
for nine days in succession 2,000 children were thus
sacrificed daily. Mexico itself never offered a picture
more horrible than the function of slaughtering these
children assigned to the Chief Sacrificator. And
whilst on common days the heavenly bodies were
to continue to be worshipped and to be honoured
by the sacrifices of beasts, it was only the Deity
who, in addition to the tribute of beasts, was to be
honoured with the tribute of children.

To overcome the difficulty of the depopulation
consequent on such a system of religion the author
made the Formosans polygamous, and the privilege

of primogeniture in the island extended for the eldest son to exemption from that liability to sacrifice which was the possible portion of all younger sons. Psalmanazar, the author, was as bold as his namesake, the prophet; the assumed credulity of the British reader being fully as remarkable as the docility of the Formosan parent. He cared nothing for existing authentic accounts of Formosa; for why should a real Formosan adjust his narrative to that of a Dutch missionary like George Candidius? If Candidius had confined the sacrifices of the Formosans to such offerings as rice and fruits, that was all very well; the British public needed stronger fare, and would be pleased with nothing short of 18,000 infants annually.

Psalmanazar admits that he deliberately made his description to clash in most particulars with the accounts of previous writers. Therefore on almost every point he contradicted Candidius. The Dutch writer had said that begging was very prevalent on the island; Psalmanazar denied that the poor were suffered to beg at all, and declared that each precinct or village had its own poorhouse. Candidius had said that there was no regular government in the island, but that at most each village was governed by twelve men of the same age, not under forty; Psalmanazar declared for an elaborate hierarchy of ministers, of whose very dress he described and depicted the minutest details. Candidius had described the laws as so lenient as to be almost non-existent;

robbery was barely punished at all, and a present of a few hogs was ample compensation for murder or adultery. According to Psalmanazar, robbers and murderers were hanged head downwards and shot to death with arrows, whilst other offences entailed burning alive, the cutting off of legs and arms, tearing in pieces by dogs, or the boring of the tongue with a hot iron. Psalmanazar had much to say of priests; Candidius only admitted the existence of priestesses.

Candidius also had denied the existence of gold or silver mines in the country; Psalmanazar made "the great quantity of gold and silver" the Formosans' chief source of profit, and located three gold and three silver mines in the several islands. Nor was this enough for British consumption, for "their temples and houses were often covered with gold, both in cities and villages". Free fancy may as well be magnificent as mean, and in keeping with these village houses of gold was the Viceroy's Palace, "three English miles in circumference".

Who could disbelieve so circumstantial a writer, capable of describing with accuracy the dress of every class in the community and of supplementing such description with woodcut illustrations? And the writer went on the principle that, the more incredible a thing was, the stronger was its title to credit. Accordingly the Formosans were said to look upon serpents as affording "very good meat and very savoury"; but how did they extract the poison? Catching the serpents alive, they would irritate them by beating them with rods; the consequent furious passion of the serpent would cause all its venom to ascend to its head, so that when this part of the body was cut off there would be no poison left in the remainder. The Formosans also carried familiar serpents about their bodies, and kept toads in their houses to purify them of infection.

Psalmanazar peopled Formosa with elephants, rhinoceroses, camels and sea-horses, "all which were tame, and very useful for the service of man". Elephants were used for drawing carts or litters, and were guided by drivers sitting on their trunks. Besides these animals were such beasts as lions, boars, wolves, leopards, apes, tigers, crocodiles and wild bulls. But the Formosans knew nothing of dragons or land-unicorns, and disbelieved in the very existence of griphons. No one seems in those days to have thought of criticising the author's zoology, which could not have been more wildly removed from the truth. For, though the zoology of Formosa is still to define with accuracy, Dr. MacKay, for twenty-three years a missionary in Formosa, only cites among the mammalia of the country such creatures as wild boars, rats, monkeys, squirrels, goats, deer, bears, ant-eaters, leopards and tiger-cats. (*From Far Formosa*, 1896, 76.)

More wonderful even than the description of Formosa were the drawings in illustration. There was the temple, with the altar and gridiron whereon the children's hearts were burnt; the different altars to the sun, moon and stars; the funeral processions; the dresses of every class and kind from the king and queen downwards to a country woman or a country bumpkin; the floating villages; the coins with their names; and above all the marvellous alphabet of twenty letters, with the names of some of them, like Lamdo and epsi, for "l" and "e," so strangely similar to the Greek Lambda and epsilon. But then they taught the Greek tongue in the academies of Formosa! As a sample of the Formosan language the author printed the Lord's Prayer, the Apostles' Creed and the Ten Commandments in Formosan words, but in Roman characters.

It seems incredible that so many of our ancestors should have been the dupes of all this. But from the first Psalmanazar had certain sceptics to deal with. Father Fontenay, the Jesuit, had been for eighteen years a missionary in Formosa, and he pointed out that Formosa was a dependency of China, not of Japan, as Psalmanazar declared; whilst Dr. Halley, the astronomer, asked the writer some unanswerable questions. Still the book had so large a sale that a second edition was published the year following, in 1705. The preface to this edition takes the highest rank in the annals of mendacity. Psalmanazar boldly therein replies to twenty-five objections "of the first magnitude" which had been raised by various critics against the statements in the first edition. On no point would he give way. At most he would say about the annual sacrifice of the 18,000 boys that such was the number laid down by the law; in practice the law might be evaded. As for the "forgeries" of Candidius, why should they be believed against the word of a native? What Candidius had said regarding maternity in Formosa was not a whit more credible than what he had said regarding the sacrifices (and this was true enough); and as to his differences from Candidius, what could more completely prove his own veracity? For surely a forger would have taken care that his statements should conform to those of previous writers. This preface of monumental audacity bears the date of the 12th of June, 1705.

The secret of Psalmanazar's success lay in the fact that he not only tickled that love for the marvellous in the British people, of which in recent times there has been a similar illustration in the adventures of De Rougemont, but also pandered to the strong feeling against the Jesuits then prevalent in England. He concluded his amazing *Description* with a sketch of the history of the Jesuits' mission to Japan, a sketch which fairly coincided with the real facts and which he made the vehicle of a strong attack upon that society, whose pupil he had been in earlier years. He adduced the great persecution of the Christians in Japan as showing "how great a prejudice the Jesuits had done to Christianity, and what a reproach and disgrace they had brought upon the

Christian name, by imposing their Popish errors upon the people as necessary articles of faith ". This and much more of the same sort was highly palatable to the British taste, and for many years this anti-Jesuit Formosan proselyte to the Church of England remained an object of faith and charity to a considerable section of his adopted countrymen.

This made it difficult for Psalmanazar to clear himself of the imposture, when he came to entertain a genuine wish to set himself right with the public. But a serious illness in 1728, and the accidental reading of Law's *Serious Call*, are said to have vanquished his irresolution, and he at once began the composition of his *Memoirs*, one of the most singular books of confession ever written. He certainly took his leisure over it, for it seems to have occupied him for twenty-five years. It was finished before 1752, when he made his first will with directions for its posthumous publication, but it did not reach the public till 1765. But long before that there had been a semi-public recantation. To Bowen's *Complete System of Geography*, published in 1747 in two large folio volumes, Psalmanazar contributed the chapters on China and Japan, and therein he dealt again with Formosa. One might suppose, he says, that Formosa had some peculiar beauty, if the account formerly given by a pretended native of it, called Psalmanazar, had had any truth in it. But that author, who was still in England, had long since owned the contrary; respect for those whom such an avowal might have injured alone prevented a public retraction; they being now dead, he gave the publishers leave to assure the world that the greater part of that account had been fabulous, and that he designed to leave behind him to be published after his death a "faithful account of that unhappy step". He then proceeded to give an account of Formosa, avowedly from Candidius, with whose account some forty years before he had deliberately made his own to clash! No wonder Formosa was a subject his friends avoided. Even Dr. Johnson avowed himself afraid of mentioning so much as China in the presence of the once-reputed Formosan.

Psalmanazar's repentance for his fraud amounted to remorse, and his self-humiliation bordered on the abject. Henceforth he would pay by voluntary self-effacement and obscurity for his earlier and wicked love for notoriety. His literary contributions should not betray his name. If he writes a most meritorious *History of Printing* for Palmer, the printer, it is published under Palmer's name as the author. If he publishes (1753) five *Essays on Miracles*, the work is attributed on the title-page to "an obscure layman in town". This is in keeping with his curious will, prefixed to his *Memoirs*, which directs that his body may be buried in some obscure corner of the common burying-ground, and uninclosed in any kind of coffin, save a shell of the lowest value, without lid or other covering to hinder the natural earth from entirely surrounding it.

Psalmanazar only obtained ten guineas for the first edition of his *Formosa*, and twelve for the second. Except for its fabulous nature, it is a work of far less interest than the *Memoirs*, which purports to be pure autobiography with nothing fabulous about it at all. It unfolds, however, an amazing story of real life that puts a severe strain on belief. The narrative seems to centre round Avignon, and therefore to justify the assumption of a French origin. But, as Psalmanazar declares that he "never met with, nor heard of any one, that ever guessed right, or anything near it, with respect to my native country," France seems to be excluded from the category of probable claimants to the honour of having produced him.

Franciscans, Jesuits and Dominicans may boast of having had each a share in the education of this extraordinary youth. And between them they taught him Latin to some effect, and something of theology. Then comes, at about the age of sixteen, a period of idleness, ending in a condition of beggary, in which condition he tramps about Europe, from his mother living somewhere apparently in France to his father living "some hundreds of miles from her"; a mysterious father who had seen the greatest part of Europe, could give an extraordinary account of it, and who understood several of its languages, but who lived in a poor house in an obscure village. Posing first as an Irishman persecuted for his religion, and then as a Formosan converted by the Jesuits to Christianity and by them conveyed to Avignon, he wanders on foot about Europe, relieving a miserable state of destitution by the alms of the charitable or the credulous. From that condition he passes into military service, and is speedily involved in the lowest depths of moral degradation, inseparable from that condition, but always passing as a Formosan, fond of theological arguments, and making an affectation of worshipping the rising or the setting sun. About two years so pass, during which, though war is raging, he sees nothing of any battle or siege, till he meets with Innes, who prevails on him to be baptised as George Lauder, and to accompany him to London to be introduced to its bishop.

Then follows the triumphant fraud, for so it must be accounted, although Psalmanazar himself admits that his "fabulous account was as much discredited by the greatest part of the world as ever". He is sent to Christ Church, he is courted in society, his book sells like wildfire. It is wonderful how a youth of twenty, pretending to be twenty-five, could sustain the part. After six months at Oxford he returns to his lodgings in Pall Mall, finds Innes flown and promoted, and brings out his second edition. From this time (1705) he confesses to ten or a dozen years "misspent in a course of the most shameless idleness, vanity and extravagance," ending in 1715 by his becoming clerk to a Lancashire regiment, his supposed Formosan nationality still procuring him easy access among "persons of rank and learning". After two years thus pleasantly spent with the regiment, passing under the nickname of "Sir George," as knighted by Queen Anne after the Peace of Utrecht, he tries to win a competence from fan-painting, but, that failing, a friendly clergyman raises an annual subscription for him, as a Formosan proselyte, of between twenty and thirty pounds a year, which large sum, together with a trifle from tuition, affords him "a comfortable competency".

Then he falls across a printer, and is set to the translating of books. From this time he leads a life as regular and studious as it had formerly been the reverse. His translations bring him "a comfortable living". He claims to have taught himself Hebrew with such success as to be able to talk it and even to compose in it. He works hard at his share of the *Universal History* or of Bowen's *Complete System of Geography;* and at such literary studies he labours happily and easily for the latter and longer part of his existence, attributing to a small nightly dose of laudanum his ability to work from 7 A.M. to 7 P.M. with "a good appetite and digestion, a clear head, and tolerable flow of spirits". And so a life that started on a fair course to the tree at Tyburn ends with the esteem of all men and the friendship of Dr. Johnson. But who Psalmanazar really was, who were his parents, and what was his country, are questions which still remain to baffle the researches of the wise or the curious. His life affords a singular instance of a career that was almost criminal being converted by determined effort into the straighter paths of industry. There are many worse texts for a good sermon than the life of Psalmanazar.

CHAPTER VI.

POLITICAL FORGERY: THE *EIKON BASILIKÉ*.

Times of great political excitement are prolific of much false literature, and the temptation to direct the course of events has at different times flooded the world with spurious writings, often with a distinct effect on the course of history. The crowning instance of a work of this nature is the famous *Eikon Basiliké*, which, appearing shortly after the execution of Charles I. as his work, contributed greatly to that reaction in his favour which in a few years culminated in the Restoration of Charles II. It may be doubted whether any book in the world's history ever had so decisive an effect on the tide of events. Burnet describes it as having enjoyed "the greatest run in many impressions" of any book of the age, and it was translated into many languages.

Yet it is evident that from its first appearance there were grave doubts as to the king's authorship of it. *The Princely Pelican* (1649) refers to contemporary reports that it was written by one of his chaplains, "to beget an esteem of learning and piety in his master as likewise to allay the rigour of the approaching sentence at Westminster" This may

possibly have been the motive of its real author, John
Gauden, then vicar of Bocking, in Essex, who, after
he had been made Bishop of Exeter in 1660, laid a
most unqualified claim to its authorship. It has been
the fashion amongst Royalist writers to treat this claim
as a pure lie on Gauden's part, and to support such
an hypothesis by unmeasured abuse (for which there
is no real foundation) of Gauden's moral character.
Wood describes Gauden as "a very comely person,
a man of vast parts"; and to call him, as Mr. Almach
does, "a cowering, craving, conceited, mean-spirited
creature," does not dispose of his claim to the authorship of the *Eikon*.

Into the vexed question of the external evidence
in favour of Charles' authorship it is needless to
enter, for, even if this were much stronger than it
has ever been shown to be, it would be entirely over-
borne by the force of the internal evidence, which is
overwhelmingly in favour of Gauden. A man can
no more escape from his style than he can from his
shadow, and so many of the literary mannerisms which
distinguish the *Eikon* distinguish also the works of
Gauden but not those of Charles, that all doubt about
the authorship seems removed by an impartial comparison.

To diminish the force of such tell-tale phrases as
show an intimate literary affinity between the *Eikon*
and Gauden, Dr. Christopher Wordsworth, Master
of Trinity College, Cambridge, the great champion
of Charles, resorted to the theory that Gauden, re-

7 *

solving shortly before the Restoration to claim the *Eikon* as his own with a view to obtain preferment, took care that his writings "subsequent to that intention should be so conformed as to render his claim the more plausible" (*Who Wrote " Eikon Basilikè " ?* iii., 111, 1824). But how can such a theory meet the case of the *Hieraspistes*, published in 1653, when no magic crystal could have foreshown the Restoration seven years afterwards? Or why should such phrases occur in Gauden's *Manual of Prayer*, a work of private devotions, which was designed for no other eyes than those of John Earle, Esquire, to whom it is dedicated, and which has never emerged from its manuscript stage in the Library at Lambeth? Or how account for such imitations of the *Eikon* in Gauden's *Religious and Loyal Protestation* of 1648 or in his four printed sermons of 1640 and 1641, when the *Eikon* did not see the light till 1649? There can be no question of borrowing here.

And if Charles' mind was the real source of such phrases as are common both to the *Eikon* and to Gauden, some indications of them should appear in the letters and other literary expressions of the royal mind, instead of being, as they are, remarkable either for their rarity or their entire absence.

With many of such phrases in common Wordsworth fenced with fair success. Those now adduced have for the most part escaped the notice of Archdeacon Todd and other believers in Gauden. They have of course a cumulative value, the case resting on a series of instances, not on single instances. Wordsworth's plan was to take a particular word or phrase, and to show that it occurred in some previous or contemporary writer as well as in the *Eikon* and in Gauden. But this does not settle the question. For the significant fact remains that these coincidences of diction occur precisely in the writer who claims the authorship of the *Eikon*, and with such frequency as to give a distinct tone to his style. It is the number of such coincidences that make it almost certain, apart from all other arguments, that Gauden and the author of the *Eikon* were one and the same person.

Gauden's fondness for metaphors amounted to a literary vice. They are drawn from every conceivable side of life, are often far-fetched, and worked out with wearisome elaboration. The remarkable thing is that most of the metaphors of the *Eikon* are identical with those which lend so peculiar a colour to Gauden's style. Gauden's metaphors may conveniently be classified under the categories of metaphors: (1) Maritime or Nautical, (2) Military, (3) Metallurgical, (4) Medical, (5) Horticultural, (6) Geometrical, (7) Igneous.

1. Maritime or nautical metaphors are among the most frequent in the *Eikon*. The author is full of the sea and storms, of helms and pilots, of ports and shipwrecks. "Lord, be Thou my pilot," he exclaims, "in this dark and dangerous storm, which neither admits my return to the port whence I set out, nor my making any other." Again: "If a pilot at sea

cannot see the polestar, it can be no fault in him to steer his course by such stars as do best appear to him". Or again : " Nor do I wish other than the safe bringing of the ship to shore, when they have cast me overboard : though it be very strange that mariners can find no other means to appease the storm themselves have raised but by drowning their pilot ".

So common a metaphor is not of course unknown to Charles, who regards the events of his time as a "great storm" or "deluge," and once alludes to himself as " Him that sits at the helm " (*Declaration*, 14th April, 1628). But the king uses such figures infrequently and in their simplest form, whereas with Gauden the use of them is unfailing and generally elaborate. He can hardly think of the State or the Church but as a ship, of which statesmen or bishops are the pilots. Let the following suffice as samples from the *Hieraspistes :* " These rustic and rash under-takers to reform and control all are only probable to shipwreck themselves, and many others, and the whole ship of this Church by driving the skilful pilots (the true bishops and ministers) from the helm, and putting in their place every bold boatswain " (114). Or : " Wise pilots know there is no point in the compass whence a tempest may not come " (117). Again : " Nor ought poor men . . . to drive, like tipsy mariners, those rightful pilots from the helm . . . that these new undertakers may try . . . how soon they can overwhelm or overcast so fair, rich and goodly vessel as this Church of England once was in the eye of all the world but our own" (129).

Similar metaphors occur in pages 31, 92, 171, 209, 526, 548 and 576. And lest it be said that Gauden acquired this literary habit from reading the *Eikon*, let it be remembered that in his first published sermon of 1640, long before the *Eikon* was thought of, he spoke of that "great cable which holds the State from shipwreck".

There would seem to be in the *Eikon* no metaphor relating to the sea which is not also in Gauden. If the *Eikon* remarks that it is better to be forced by sea to a storm than to venture "splitting or sinking *on a lee shore*," Gauden is not far behind when he speaks of ministers "whom for the most part necessity drives into this port of the ministry, and there keeps them so under hatches or *on the lee* that they are seldom able to adventure," etc. (*Hps.*, 497).

Gauden bids princes and governors "set banks and boundaries" to the common people "as to great waters" (*Hps.*, 117); he speaks of "those to whose rage, as to seas, the Lord hath hitherto set bounds" (*ib.*, 33); "which were never wont to overflow the constant banks of the divinely established calling of the Ministry, but still were kept within those holy and humble bounds" (220). He cannot get his mind away from overflowing seas: "As the sea by modest lickings and slidings over the *banks* which afterwards its fury *overbears* with horrible inundations". The habit might not be worth remarking but for the manifestation of the same habit by the author of the *Eikon*, who exclaims : " Thou canst soon cause the overflowing seas to ebb, and retire back again to the bounds which Thou hast appointed them," and who complains of " these popular inundations which Thou permittest to *overbear* all the *banks* of loyalty and modesty ". It is visible at a glance how both writers dress identically the same thought in identically the same words ; as we should expect them to do if Gauden wrote for the king.

2. Military metaphors furnish another category which displays the same correspondence between the thought and words of Gauden and of Charles.

Foul and false aspersions, says Charles, " were *secret engines* at first employed against my people's love of me, that, *undermining* their opinion and value of me, my enemies, and theirs too, might at once blow up their affections and batter down their loyalty ". Or again : " where many *engines* of religious and fair pretensions are brought chiefly to *batter* or ease episcopacy ".

Gauden comes very near this when he compares persecutions to " the Devil's engines *to batter or undermine* the Church of Christ " (462), or complains that " there are now not only *secret underminings* but *open engines* " (34).

The real Charles once speaks of a Parliamentary measure as an " engine " (*Basilika*, ii., 152), and refers to his enemies as *undermining* a wall and shaking foundations (*ib.*, ii., 137), but these can hardly weigh against the remarkable antithesis between the "secret engines" of the *Eikon* and the "open engines" of the *Hieraspistes*. Nor can it be thought that Gauden borrowed the metaphor from Charles, for in his sermon of 1640 we find him saying : "There is no *engine* you can invent so effectual to *batter down* and demolish the adverse party" (24) ; which shows a fondness for these words long prior to the appearance of the *Eikon*.

Under this head of military metaphors the *Eikon's* allusion to "*the forked arrow* of factious emulation" may be compared with Gauden's phrase, "Another great calamity . . . is as a *forked arrow*" (*Hps.*, 321), or "carrying with them in their festered consciences the *forked arrow*," etc. (*Bloody Slaughter-house*, 51).

3. Metallurgical metaphors afford another closely connecting link between Charles and Gauden. Out of four allusions to furnaces in the *Eikon* one may be quoted : "Never were princes more glorious than those whom God hath suffered to be tried in the *furnace of affliction*" ; with which may be compared this from Gauden : "Nor shall this *furnace of affliction* be to consume this Reformed Church, but only to purge her," etc. (*Hps.*, 99) ; or again : "When they are red-hot in the *forge of affliction*, and hammered on the anvils of the world's malice" (390).

Or compare the words of the *Eikon*, "bring us at last *more refined* out of these fires," with such a passage in Gauden's *Prayer Manual* as "make Thy Church and faithful servants, both ministers and people, even to be as Thy gold, in Thy furnace, not less precious to Thee, but more fitted, because *more refined* for Thy service"; or with the passage in the *Hieraspistes* where Gauden writes of the Deity as "casting His gold into the hottest furnace to make it at once more pure in itself and more precious to Himself" (561).

And here is another tell-tale metaphor derived from smelting. "Some men thought," says the *Eikon*, "that the Government of this Church and State . . . would not *run into their new moulds* till they had first *melted* it in the fire of a civil war". Gauden had a special love for this phrase. " Nothing more easily *runs into new moulds* . . . than many ministers do" (*Hps.*, 521); "Is he angry that preachers . . . are not presently *melted* with every popular glowing heat of seeming piety? and that they *run into any mould*," etc. (222). And again he refers to the "hotter *meltings* of any bolder Independents who made religion and reformation *run to any new moulds* which they fancy" (*Hps.*, Pref., 3). And references to pages 417, 522, 578, 587, will further show how essential a part of Gauden's mental furniture was this resort to metallurgical metaphors, which are altogether foreign to the mind of Charles.

4. Medical metaphors abound of course in all writers, and even in the writings of Charles diseases and distempers, cures and physicians, play their natural part. But in Gauden such metaphors are so frequent as to disfigure his style. They are also of

wearisome frequency in the *Eikon;* but it is the perpetual antithesis between *poison and antidote* which is so striking a common feature of both Gauden and the author of the *Eikon.*

From many passages in Gauden the following may suffice as illustrations: "As good laws oft rise by the occasion of evil manners, like *antidotes from poisons*" (*Hps.*, 209); or from the *Prayer Manual:* "Give me . . . the antidote of charity against the poison of other injuries". In a similar way the *Eikon:* "As our sins have turned our *antidotes into poisons,* so let Thy grace turn our *poisons into antidotes*"; or again: "Let mine and other men's constancy be an *antidote* against the *poison* of their example". Charles uses the word "antidote" three times in his undoubted works, but never in contrast with "poison," as was the habit of Gauden.

5. Horticultural metaphors form another distinctive feature of Gauden's style, and more especially the Pauline metaphor of "planting and watering". The following are but a few instances out of many. In his sermon of 29th November, 1640, he asks: "Have we so long been a vine *planted and watered* and fenced?" In his *Prayer Manual:* "Restore Thy Church . . . which heretofore so happily *planted, watered,* and preserved," etc. In the *Hieraspistes:* "Ministers . . . who may be always either *planting, or watering,* or pruning" (185); "fair flowers of Christ's *planting and watering*" (112); "whose stock first *planted and watered* in the universities" (386).

And in his *Cromwell's Bloody Slaughter-house*, written in February, 1649, we again find the phrase "*watered* with the blood of the King and his subjects" (104).

Of course any writer was free to use the phrase, but Charles never uses it: which fact makes its recurrence in the *Eikon* highly significant. "If Presbytery in such a supremacy be an institution of Christ, sure it differs from all others, and is the first and only point of Christianity which was to be *planted and watered* with so much Christian blood." Or again: "Thy vineyard which Thy right hand hath *planted* and *the dew of heaven watered* to a happy and flourishing estate". Gauden's expression "plentifully *watered with the dew of heaven*" (*Hps.*, 386) throws light on this last passage as well as on the following in the *Eikon*: "All ministers will find as great a difference in point of thriving between the favour of the People and of Princes, as plants do between being *watered* by hand, or by the sweet and liberal *dews of Heaven*".

How can all these resemblances be better accounted for than by the theory that they were all written by Gauden?

6. The author of the *Eikon* had also a special love for geometrical metaphors. Circles, centres and lines had for him an unfailing attraction. Thus he writes of "notions which go rather in and round a circle of fancy than in a *right line* of reason tending to the law, the only centre of public consistency"; he notices

how impossible it is "for lines to be drawn from the
centre, and not to divide from each other, so much
the wider, by how much they go farther from the
point of union"; and he trusts, for the Prince of
Wales, that to the "centre of true happiness (*i.e.*, his
salvation) God hath and will graciously direct those
black lines of affliction, which he hath pleased to draw
on himself".

In the reported conference at Raglan Castle between Charles and the Marquis of Worcester the
King is made to speak of the Greek Church as the
"centre and circumference" of the Catholic Church,
and he once speaks of a "circle of order" (*Bibliotheca
Regia*, i., 100); but this amounts to very little. The
metaphor is not part and parcel of his style, as it is of
Gauden's. Compare with the above passages from
the *Eikon* the following from the *Hieraspistes* :—

"All gifts . . . of God's spirit . . . are in all
motions, habits, and operations as conform to the
Scriptures as any *right line* is to that rule by which
it is drawn" (327).

"So far are those lines which the anti-ministerial
fury and folly draws from moving parallel to piety or
Christianity . . . that they are most diametrically
opposite to all civility" (Pref., 33). Christians are
"*lines* drawn from several points of faith's circumference, yet to the same centre, Jesus Christ" (455).

And lest it be said that Gauden caught this love
for geometry from the *Eikon*, the sermon he preached
before Parliament on 29th November, 1640, may again

be quoted to show that Gauden had acquired the habit of thinking in terms of geometry long before there was an *Eikon* to imitate. "Truth is but one, as the centre," he says, "and draws all minds to an unity which tends to it" (41).

7. But it is the metaphor igneous that more conclusively than all others establishes the identity of Gauden and the author of the *Eikon*. Gauden's pages fairly scintillate with "sparks" and "flames" and "fires," just as also scintillate the pages of the *Eikon*, but not the pages of the genuine Charles.

As samples of this habit the following may be quoted from the *Eikon* :—

"What flames of discontent this spark soon kindled all the world is witness."

"The brands of that fire, being ill quenched, have kindled the like flames here."

"In whose hearts they seek by all means to smother and extinguish all sparks of love, respect and loyalty to me."

"Not the least incentive that kindled and blew up into those horrid flames the sparks of discontent."

These are only a few instances of a habit which gives a distinct colouring to the *Eikon*. It is therefore significant that precisely the same colouring is given to all Gauden's works by his constant resort to the same metaphor. Here are a few illustrations :—

"The sparks of many men's passionate opinions . . . at last lighting upon thatched houses . . . have set their own houses on fire" (*Hps.*, 33).

" How fain would some that the sun were set that their glow-worms might shine ; that the light of the house were extinguished ; that so their sparks might appear which they have kindled to themselves " (*Hps.*, 396).

" Every novelty of fashion in religion . . . puts out Thy sacred sparks and embers in Christian hearts, yea, and kindles those unholy . . . fires of contrariety, jealousy, . . . to so great heights of all-devouring flames," etc. (*Hps.*, 133).

These are from Gauden's *Life of Hooker*(1661):—

" They conspired to kindle those *horrid fires* of civil war which this wise author foresaw and foretold in his admirable preface which follow those sparks and that smoke which he saw rise in his days " (see *" horrid flames "* in *Eikon*, 12).

" If by any means he might extinguish those fires whose smokings he already felt and whose flames he feared would at last break out to dreadful conflagrations."

In the sermons, too, which he preached long before the *Eikon* was written, there is the same unfailing love for the igneous metaphor :—

" Like powder we kindle upon the least spark of offence and instantly flame to revenge " (Oxford, 11th July, 1641).

" Where the coals of private dissensions are scattered in every corner, the whole house will soon be on fire " (Chelmsford, 1641).

If we now turn from categories of corresponding

metaphors in the *Eikon* and in Gauden, and take single metaphors, the same amazing affinity is ever before us.

There is that metaphor from archery in the curious phrase of the *Eikon :* "A great part of whose piety *hung upon that popular pin* of railing against and condemning the Government". Gauden supplies a similar passage : "The weight of Christianity doth not at all *hang on this popular pin,*" etc. (*Hps.*, 116).

Sometimes the metaphor is from bowls. Compare in the *Eikon* "that nothing of passion shall have any *bias upon my judgment*" with Gauden's "that partial *bias on their judgment* which shall mar all their learning" (*Hps.*, 287).

Sometimes the metaphor is from tennis. Says the *Eikon :* "People's *rebounds* are oft in their faces, who first put them on those violent strokes". Gauden writes : "I have done with the first part of this cavil or calumny which seeks to bandy the Church of England against the Papal or Romish *wall;* that they may make it either *rebound* to a popular or Independent side, or else fall into the *hazard* of having no true Christian ministry at all" (*Hps.*, 259).

Poultry-rearing supplies the author of the *Eikon* with "*proud* and arrogant activity which seeks to *hatch every egg* of different *opinions* to a faction or schism". And it is Gauden who writes: "How lothe are vain and *proud* men to think the *egg* of any *opinions* which they have laid or *hatched* to be addled" (505).

Always in the *Eikon* and in Gauden this strange use of the same thought in the same words. If the *Eikon* speaks of "the differences in lesser matters which are but the skirts and *suburbs of religion*," it is Gauden who supplies the parallel : " If in lesser things which are but the lace and fringe of the holy vestment, the verge and *suburbs of religion*" (*Hps.*, 453), and who writes in his *Prayer Manual* of "*the suburbs* of hell ".

The *Eikon* has it : " My prayer to God is . . . that He would be pleased to make you an *anchor* or harbour rather to these *tossed* and weather-beaten kingdoms"; and Gauden writes : " Christians must not always be *tossing* to and fro in religion, but come to an *anchor* of fixation " (*Hps.*, 452).

The *Eikon* is fond of such a figure as "to *see this sin in the glass* of their punishment "; with which compare in Gauden's *Religious and Loyal Protestation* of 5th January, 1649 : " I would rather you should *see your sins in such glasses* of free and fair remonstrance ". Or compare from the *Eikon :* " Make our sins appear to our consciences as they are *represented in the glass* of Thy judgments," with Gauden's description of human affairs as "most fully *represented in the glass* of our times " (*Hps.*, 528).

" Forgive their sins . . . who have deserved Thy just punishment thus to let in the *wild boar . . . to waste and deform Thy vineyard*". So the *Eikon ;* and so Gauden writes of certain persons who "like

8

so many *wild boars* sought *to lay waste the Lord's vineyard*" (*Hps.*, 54).

Gauden loved these comparisons of men with animals.   He writes of those "*swine* which . . . root up the pastures, break through the fences and waste the corn" (*Hps.*, 457), and so the *Eikon :* "As *swine* are to gardens and orderly plantations, so are tumults to Parliaments".

There is the phrase in the *Eikon :* "The tuition of kings and queens which have been *nursing fathers and mothers* of this Church," and Gauden has : "This Church which by the princely piety of *nursing fathers and mothers* hath been so long preserved" (*Hps.*, 99).   The phrase is from Isaiah xlix. 23.

The *Eikon* has a metaphor from carpentry : "Nor is it so proper to *hew* out religious reformations by the sword as to *polish* them by fair and religious disputations".   And so Gauden says of the Schoolmen that they rather "*hewed* and cut the pillars of Christian religion into small chips and shavings than added much to the *polishing* and establishing of them" (*Hps.*, 401).

The best explanation of all these resemblances of phrase is the unity of the mind that produced them. Dr. Wordsworth had a simple theory for disposing of them : if they occurred in a work by Gauden of later date than the *Eikon*, then they were derived from the *Eikon ;* if they occurred in a work of earlier date than the *Eikon*, then Charles, a great reader of sermons, had derived them from the sermons of

Gauden. But this is special pleading of the commonest sort, which can convince no one. Dr. Wordsworth's theory was that Gauden intentionally copied the *Eikon* in order to press his claim to its authorship with more plausibility. But in Gauden's claim, made to Lord Clarendon, there is no reference to such coincidences as proof of such authorship, and it is idle to think of a man writing a long book like the *Hieraspistes* on the chance of its supporting a claim not to be made till seven years afterwards, and then only on the chance of a complete political revolution. And is it not ridiculous to think of a man of affairs like the Chancellor wading through all Gauden's voluminous works in order to convince himself that Gauden's claim was a veracious one? Lord Clarendon of course knew that it was true on other grounds, and never controverted it.

But besides sameness of metaphors, there are certain favourite phrases and antitheses which further establish the truth of Gauden's claim.

1. The antithesis between the "just" and the "unjust".

In the *Eikon* we have, "whose *just* recovery of their rights from *unjust* usurpations," or, "which his *justice* by the very *unjust* hands of some of my subjects". Charles in a letter to the queen (14th Nov., 1646) alludes to the "*unjust justice*" of Parliament, but Gauden comes nearer to the *Eikon* with his "that which you call *justice* against the King seems to me the greatest and most unparalleled *injustice*"

8 *

(*Religious Protestation*, 1649), or "the *unjust* exe-
cutioners of the *just* vengeance" (*Slaughter-house*, 9),
or "a new court of *justice* (as men *unjustly* term it)"
(*ib.*, 24).

2. The antithesis between "intend" and "pretend". The *Eikon* has : "How they keep their
covenants in point of piety *pretended*, provided they
adhere firmly to the party and design *intended*".
So Gauden to Lord Fairfax and the General Council
of War in his *Religious and Loyal Protestation* of
5th January, 1649 : "Let not the world find in the
event that your *pretended* mercies were *intended*
cruelties".

3. The antithesis between "word" and "sword".
The *Eikon* has a special love for playing off these
words against each other. "In vain is my person
excepted by a parenthesis of *words* when so many
hands are armed against me with *swords*."

Again : "Whose *words* were sometimes smoother
than oil, but now I see they would prove very
swords".

Again : "More glorious to convert souls to God's
Church by the *word* than to conquer men to subjec-
tion by the *sword*".

Or again : "Destroy myself by my *word* or not
suffer them to do it unresisted by the *sword*".

Gauden has the same partiality for the same
antithesis :—

"Our *words* are sharp *swords* daily whetting or
clashing against each other" (*Hps.*, 139) ; "so as the

ministry directs the magistracy by the *word* and the magistracy assists the ministry by the *sword*" (*Hps.*, 400); "if arguments and *words* could not, yet arms and *swords* have, they say, convinced the bishops" (*ib.*, 260).

4. The antithesis between "use" and "abuse".

Not an uncommon antithesis, but again one which happens to be a favourite both with Gauden and the writer of the *Eikon*. In the *Eikon* we read: "Make me so far happy as to make a right *use* of others' *abuses*".

"To know how to sever between the *use and abuse* of things."

"The *abuses* of which deserve to be extirpated as much as the *use* retained."

From eight instances in the *Hieraspistes* may be quoted:—

"Least able to distinguish between the *abuse and use* of things" (302).

"Much more folly it is quite to abolish the *use* of holy things than to tolerate some *abuses* with it" (256).

"The soldiery might *use* or rather *abuse* their helmets" (34).

And Gauden loved the antithesis long before the *Eikon*, for in his sermon of 1640 he speaks of those "who seek to *abuse* antiquity by *using* those names," etc.

5. The antithesis between "ending" and "mending," which has recently become famous in a political reference.

In the *Eikon* we have : " I had the charity to interpret that most part of my subjects . . . intended to *mend me, not to end me* ".   And so Gauden in the Preface to his *Hieraspistes :* " If it be the *mending, not the ending* . . . of ministers which their severe censurers and opposers seek for ".

6. The antithesis between " please " and " displease ".

From the *Eikon* comes : " It is too much that they have once overcome me, to *please* them by *displeasing* Thee ".

And : " If I may be happy to *please* Thee, I need not fear whom I *displease* ".

Again it is Gauden who loves the same : " It will be hard to *please* any one without *displeasing* many " (Pref., *Hps.*).

" If they do but *please* themselves, it matters not how they *displease* God " (505).

" To *please* myself in what I could not but think very *displeasing* to Thee " (*Manual of Prayer*) ; and " as may never make my *pleasure* Thy *displeasure* " (*ib.*).

7. The antithesis between " piety " and " policy ".

Though Fuller or others may use the same antithesis, it is one that must be noticed as another literary link between Gauden and the *Eikon*.   Compare in the *Eikon* " whom it most concerns *both in piety and policy,*" or " not so much out of *piety as policy,*" with the following from Gauden : " a matter of policy rather than piety " (*Hps.*, 280) ; " rather a common act of reason and *polity* as men than proper to them as Christians in *piety*" (*Hps.*, 300); "no less necessity *both in piety and policy*" (*ib.*, 233); "that human *policy* may not overcome true *piety*" (*Manual*); "however differing in some principles rather of *polity* than *piety*" (Letter to Bernard).

The case for Gauden is further strengthened by reference to certain uncommon words or conjunction of words. "The Independents," says the *Eikon*, "think themselves *manumitted* from their rivals' services." So Gauden writes of novices in the ministry "which have but lately been *manumitted* from the rod and ferule" (*Hps.*, 27).

"So slight and easy," says the *Eikon*, "is that *legerdemain* which will serve to delude the vulgar"; and so Gauden talks of "those pretty *legerdemains* in religion" (*Hps.*, 323).

The *Eikon* speaks of the "*perplexed labyrinths* of our own thoughts". Gauden is fond of the word "labyrinth," and once writes of the "*labyrinth* . . . of *perplexed* designs" (*Slaughter-house*, 45).

"Ambitious minds never think they have laid *snares and gins* enough," says the *Eikon*; "that so none might discover his *snares and gins*," says Gauden (*Hps.*, 395).

"As *showers* do follow *warm gleams*," has the *Eikon*; with which compare from Gauden: "Yet should these *warmer gleams* in ministers' hearts rather have vented themselves in soft dews and sweet *showers* than in lightnings" (*Hps.*, 25).

Connecting in the same way the *Eikon* with Gauden is the use of such words as "smother and overlay," "rust and dross," "many-headed hydra," "the itch of novelty," "tumultuary violence," "touchstone," "the light of reason and religion," "prone," and the tiresome repetition of the expression "some men". Doubtless these expressions belonged more or less to the literary stock of the time, but the large number of coincidences between the style of Gauden and the author of the *Eikon* cannot be gainsaid, nor easily explained away. Dr. Wordsworth asserted that "no one ever had pointed out, or could point out, any one sentence or word, tending in the slightest degree to substantiate or warrant" Gauden's claim; it can only be replied that either his two perusals of the *Hieraspistes* were inexcusably superficial or that they were attended by a predetermination to find no evidence that ran counter to a preconceived theory. The real truth is that the *Eikon* is a sort of literary mosaic of Gaudenian expressions, and that there is hardly a thought in the *Eikon* that is foreign to Gauden.

And often this thought is clothed in the closest possible similarity of words. Here, for instance, is a passage from the *Eikon* of which the italicised words deserve to be closely compared with a passage from Gauden : "For those *secular* additaments and ornaments of authority . . . which my predecessors . . . have annexed to bishops and churchmen, I look upon them but as just *rewards of their learning*, and piety . . . meet strengthenings of their *authority* and observance. . . . I would have such men bishops who are most worthy of these *encouragements.*"

Gauden also writing of bishops, says : " I do not much consider the *secular* parade and equipage further than as public *encouragements* of merit, as excitations to excel, as noble *rewards of learning*, and as extern decencies or solemnities which do much set off and embroider *authority* in the sight of the vulgar " (*Hps.*, 274).

Again, the whole of Gauden's long argument of the proper relations between Episcopacy and Presbytery is identical with that of the *Eikon.* One reason Gauden gives for preferring Episcopacy is "the avoiding of *scandal*-giving to so many Christian churches, remaining in all the world : who, for the major part, are still governed by bishops, in some respects distinct from and eminent above the presbyters : it is not the work of .Christian prudence or *charity to widen differences* between us and other churches " (*Hps.*, 265). The *Eikon* uses many of the same words to express the same thought : " Nor is it any point of wisdom or *charity* where Christians differ (as many do in some parts) there to *widen the differences*, and at once to give the Christian world (except a handful of some Protestants) so great a *scandal* in point of Church government ".

Again, " I should be glad," says Gauden, "to see the *counsel* and assistance of well-settled presbyters crowned with the order and lustre of episcopal *presidency* ". Says the *Eikon*, closely following :

" Not that I am against the managing of this *pre-sidency* and authority in one man by the joint *counsel* and consent of many presbyters ".

It would be tedious to quote more passages revealing affinities which go deeper than the mere expression of ideas and touch the very ideas themselves. For Wordsworth's theory of Gauden's moral and spiritual incapacity to have written the *Eikon* there is not the smallest foundation. The *Hieraspistes* abounds with passages not one whit spiritually inferior to those of the *Eikon*. There are passages in praise of Charity, of Holiness, of Forgiveness not only equal to anything in the *Eikon* but strangely similar in tone. Unhappily the scurrilous and the spiritual jostle one another somewhat painfully in Gauden's writings, but it is unfair to collect these darker utterances as if they stood alone, and then contrast them with the best passages of the *Eikon*. Yet this simple trick of controversy has been the favourite weapon of Charles' partisans from Dr. Wordsworth to Mr. Almach.

Mr. Scott, in support of Charles, has quoted as very similar to the terse and epigrammatic sentences of the *Eikon* certain apophthegmata in Charles' own handwriting in his copy at the British Museum of Bacon's *Advancement of Learning*; as, for example, " Temperance rewards a man when he least thinks of it," or " How can that be a virtue which is built upon vice ? " But the *Hieraspistes* supplies abundant and more applicable sentences, as " God oft hangs great weights on little wires, and sets great wheels

on work by little springs" (37); "Human disgraces
are oft the foils and whetstones of divers graces"
(565); "Tithes, like molehills in an evening sun, cast
long shadows from little heights" (494); "O Father
of Lights . . . let our moment here be sincere love
to Thyself, perfect charity to Thy Church, and holy
humanity to all men" (141). These are some of
many sentences in Gauden which in tone and manner
are absolutely in unison with passages in the *Eikon*.

Thus the literary case for Gauden is so strong
that it can only be met by an equally strong case on
behalf of Charles. But is this possible? Here and
there in the works of Charles one catches a phrase
or thought which recalls the *Eikon*. The rather uncommon word "Boutefeu" for an incendiary, which
occurs once in the *Eikon*, occurs twice in his works
(*Bas.*, ii., 178, and *Bib. Regia*, ii., 64), but I have
failed to find it in Gauden. The recurring references
in the *Eikon* to Honour and Conscience are in complete accordance with similar references in the king's
letters to the queen, to the Duke of Ormonde, and
in some of his public papers. His letter to the Prince
of Wales of 29th November, 1648, and his Declaration of 18th January, 1647, and of 22nd November,
1648, are quite in the spirit of the *Eikon*, but from
some of these, or similar sources, the composer of
the *Eikon* might have drawn some of his inspira-
tion. There is, however, in the real or alleged
works of the king a marked absence of those many
curious words, metaphors and antitheses which form

so conspicuous a feature of Gauden's style and of the style of the author of the *Eikon*. However much therefore one may admire Charles for his fine spirit of placability and patience, however much one may deplore his fate, the claims of truth compel one irresistibly to the conclusion that the *Eikon* has no real right to the title of "the King's Book," but that it must be assigned "wholly and only" to the invention of Gauden.

Others of course must have been privy with Gauden to the imposture, and kept the secret to themselves. If Dugard's affidavit, entered in the Record Office under the date of October, 1661, may be trusted, Dugard printed it as "the King's Book," having received it from Symmons, the king's chaplain; and at the same time he received to print (though it was not printed till later) a work by Gauden sent to him from the Hague by Sir E. Nicholas (28th April, 1649). There was in all this some plot or trickery which cannot now be explained ; for, according to the Stationer's Court Record, on 2nd April, 1649, Symmons came before the Court with a request that the entrance to him of the King's Book might be "crossed out and made void, which was granted, and he did it with his own hand and subscribed his name thereto". What can this mean but that Symmons, having been made party to a fraud, wished to clear himself of complicity in it, and that he refused to have anything to do with its appellation of "the King's Book"?

But Gauden's work cannot fairly be classed amongst ordinary forgeries. In his endeavour to write in the spirit of the king he so far surpassed himself as to produce a masterpiece in its kind. Allowance, too, must be made for the effect on a strong and sincere loyalist of the dire extremity of the king's condition. If by such means a diversion might be created in his favour, how can the idea and the attempt be blamed? Gauden in a sense re-created Charles I., and the Royalists of to-day, instead of covering Gauden with abuse, should more rightfully raise a statue to his memory.

CHAPTER VII.

FORGERY IN THE CHURCH.

FORGERY, which has invaded every department of literary activity, has made its most complete conquests and left its most indelible marks in the field of ecclesiastical literature. The composition of works in support of definite ends, though it long preceded the Christian era, seems to have acquired increased impetus after the introduction of the new religion had supplied new motives for fictitious writing. The contest from the first between different opinions and doctrines led naturally to works composed in defence of the writer's views, and to their ascription to names which might serve to claim attention and to clothe them with credit.

The consequence has been the hopeless bewilderment of critics of a later date who have vainly attempted to separate the wheat from the chaff, and to distinguish between the genuine and spurious works of the early Christian Church.

A final judgment can never be hoped for regarding such productions as the letters attributed to St. Clement, St. Ignatius, or Polycarp, nor is the mystery likely to be solved as to the authorship of the *Sibyl-line Oracles*, the *Correspondence of St. Paul and Seneca*, or those books of the New Testament which Eusebius placed in his category of Contested Scriptures.

When forgery became ecclesiastical, it touched the infinite. The greatness of the interests at stake, the rivalries of doctrines and churches, produced for an insatiable demand a boundless supply of false documents. False epistles and false martyrdoms entered so widely into the history of the Christian Church as to have rendered that history mainly hypothetical.

Even into the earliest and most honest attempt at such a history, that of Eusebius in the fourth century, much that is fabulous has found its way. The correspondence between Christ and Agbar, King of Edessa, has long been relegated to the realm of fiction, though accepted as genuine by Eusebius; and it may be suspected that as little credit is due to such an episode as that of the Martyrs of Lyons which he relates in his fifth book as illustrative of a world-wide persecution under Marcus Aurelius in the year 177. For no writer, pagan or Christian, before him makes the least allusion to such an event, and Eusebius lived about a century and a half after its alleged occurrence. It is incredible that contemporaries like Tertullian (about 150-240), Clement of Alexandria (150-220), Athenagoras, Origen (185-234), or other intermediate writers like

Cyprian or Lactantius, all six of whom wrote specifically on the subject of persecutions, should have conspired to make not the smallest allusion to any persecution of the sort, had such a persecution been an historical reality.

Tradition has always connected the name of Irenæus, Presbyter of Lyons at the time, with the authorship of this narrative, and the tradition is amply supported by the style of the composition. As he represents the pagans as searching out even the most obscure Christians, it is not evident how so prominent a Christian as himself incurred no danger at all, but remained an uninjured spectator of the persecution, and was suffered to hold free intercourse with the martyrs in prison. But this is only one of the many difficulties. And a writer who could assert, as Irenæus did, that he himself had often heard persons "speak with tongues," and that it was a common thing in the church of his day to raise the dead to life again, has no claim to the unlimited belief that has been vouchsafed to him. He was probably one of the earliest composers of those fictitious Martyria which became so favourite a subject with imaginative writers. And there is strong evidence that he also wrote the story of the martyrdom of Polycarp and others at Smyrna (for which an equivocal allusion by himself is the only contemporary evidence with the smallest claim to value). Irenæus has no title to implicit trust when he relates martyrdoms to which no satisfactory date can be assigned, and which conflict at innumerable points with all that is otherwise known of the history of the time.

No denial of the numerous and cruel persecutions of the early Christians which have blackened the pages of history is involved in the proposition that in no other direction did exaggeration and invention become more conspicuous. Such Martyria were the form that pious fiction took. On the accepted principle that that must be the truth for which men had been willing to die, martyrdoms were regarded as the best proof of soundness of doctrine. Origen's clear statement, that down to his time those who had actually died for the faith were very few and easily numerable, (though attempts have been made to reduce its significance), really governs all the cases of martyrdom recorded of the first two centuries.

And as the centuries continued, these fictions increased in volume, till at last we reach that Bollandist collection in sixty-four colossal volumes which it took many generations of Jesuit writers more than 150 years to complete, from the time when John Bollandus began the work : perhaps the most astonishing literary enterprise that the world can show, though certainly as historically worthless as it is wonderful in execution.

In the gradual course of the contest between varying shades of Christian thought certain books came to be distinguished as genuine or canonical as opposed to others which were apocryphal. When the necessity of a rule of faith became obvious, as it did

9

towards the end of the second century, about the time
of Irenæus, certain books were accepted to supply
and constitute the Canon, and certain others were
excluded from it. The grounds for such exclusion
are no longer clear, and several works, now deemed
apocryphal, enjoyed for a time the sunshine of the
Church's favour. As a rule apocryphal works were
ascribed to heretics, but this only meant that they
were the work of an ecclesiastical minority. Sometimes even the writer belonged to the orthodox and
dominant party, as in the case of that unnamed Presbyter of the Church who, according to Irenæus, was
the author of the *Acts of Paul and Thecla*.

It is only rarely that a name emerges in those
early times. Pope Innocent I. (A.D. 402-417), in his
reference to uncanonical works, condemns those
circulated under the name of St. Andrew as the
works of two philosophers, called Nexocharides and
Leonidas; whilst others under the names of St.
Matthias or James the Less, of St. Peter and John
(exclusive of the canonical works), he assigns to a
certain Leutius. This Leutius is probably the same
person who is referred to again in Pope Galasius
list of apocryphal books, where he alludes to " the
Gospels which Lucianus falsified" and to " all the
books made by Lucius, disciple of the devil ". Esitius
is also mentioned as another writer of these false
Gospels.

Galasius, quoting from memory, makes a goodly
list of works which had an heretical or a schismatic

origin.   It is curious to find in a list containing such works as "the Acts of St. Andrew; of St. Thomas; of St. Philip," or "the Gospels of St. Matthias; of St. Peter; of St. James ; of St. Barnabas; or St. Bartholomew," the works also of such pillars of the Church as Tertullian, Lactantius and Arnobius.

The principle on which the Church rejected some works and received others is lost to us, and it would be an endless task to try to test the justice of the decision.   It is evident that an overwhelming mass of fiction was produced which tried to win a footing in the world under the cloak of certain distinguished Christian names.   The motives of the writers may be fairly well divined, but their names are for the most part as little known to us as they were probably to their contemporaries.

But all other ecclesiastical forgeries pale before that of the "False Decretals," compared with which the worst frauds from other fields of literature seem but paltry and almost venial.   These others may have served to enrich an impostor or to bewilder the learned, but the "False Decretals" affected and still affect the history of the world and the destinies of nations.   They enjoyed an undisputed authority and an unsuspected title from their first appearance about the middle of the ninth century to the fifteenth, when the suspicion of their fictitious character rapidly passed into certainty.

The attempt to impose them on the world as the work of Isidore, the learned Archbishop of

Seville who died in 636, was most deliberate; for the preface purports to be by Isidore, and is continued as if by him in the first person singular. And the ruse was perfectly successful, for who in that age would venture to gainsay the authority of Isidore?

The immense literature which has been built upon the "False Decretals" has failed to detect with certainty their real author. They have been assigned by some with a fair show of reason to Ebo, who preceded Hincmar as Archbishop of Rheims; by some to Otgar, Archbishop of Mainz; by some to Rothad, Bishop of Soissons, whom they helped Pope Nicholas I. to defend against Hincmar; by some to Benedictus Levita, Deacon of Mainz. Amid such diversity of opinion the only bond of agreement seems to exist in their ascription to some ecclesiastic of prominent position in the Church. It was a churchman's, not a layman's production.

The unknown writer of the "Decretals" did not rely entirely on his own powers of invention, but made extensive use of genuine earlier documents. Thus the second part of his work, consisting of the Canons of the Greek, African, Gallic and Spanish Councils to the year 683, was incorporated from the "Hispana Collectio" of Councils, collected about the end of the seventh century, and also ascribed erroneously to Isidore, Archbishop of Seville. And this in its turn was based on an earlier collection made in the sixth century by Dionysius Exiguus, who is famous as having been the first to introduce the Christian era into chronology.

But the mass of spurious work is nevertheless amazing. The sixty Decretals or Rescripts of the first part, extending from Pope Clement in the first century to Melchiades in the fourth, and distributed among twenty-nine different Popes, constitute a remarkable literary performance. And yet of these letters Dionysius Exiguus, who lived at Rome, strange to say, knew nothing.

But this is not all. For the third part, which includes many genuine letters taken from the " Hispana Collectio," and covers the period from Pope Sylvester in the fourth century to Gregory II. in the eighth, contains as many as thirty-five forged letters, including all to the time of Pope Damasus, namely, those of Sylvester, Marcus, Julius, Liberius and Felix. And even the genuine letters suffer from interpolations.

The whole thing was contrived and composed with the greatest ability. The writer covers the whole field of Christian doctrine, morals and discipline, and an irreproachable Papal style and elevated moral tone never deserts him. Excellent sermons might to this day be culled from the " False Decretals," dealing as they often do with the commonest stumbling-blocks of daily life. As where, for example, Pope Fabian (A.D. 242) says : " Many have perished by the sword, but more there are who have perished through their own tongue ".

And the same words are put into the mouth of

Pope Pontianus (A.D. 230); in fact, a whole page of
Pope Pontianus is almost verbally identical with a
passage in Pope Fabian, as if the writer thought that
a passage to his liking could not appear too often ; or
as if he forgot, in composing a letter for Pope Fabian,
that he had already used the same passage in composing,one for Pope Pontianus.   Such repetitions are
not infrequent in his work, and, supplementing long
quotations from the Bible, must have much facilitated
the task of composition.

The " False Decretals " constituted as it were an
additional storey in an edifice of falsehood.   It is difficult to say at how early a date the wilful falsification
of history for ecclesiastical purposes began ; but a
vigorous attempt in this direction had already been
made in the sixth century when the catalogue of the
Roman bishops, the *Liber Pontificalis*, appeared in its
first edition of 530.   The fictions in this work about
the Popes, whom it represented as always legislating
for the Church as a whole, were incorporated in the
" False Decretals," and in those uncritical times
helped to give support to the later fabrication.

It has been contended that the " False Decretals "
rather expressed the Christianity of the ninth century
than added anything material to Christian tradition.
In any case the work was not produced without a
very definite object, and the object that clearly interested its composer more than any other was the advancement of the episcopate, and of the interests of
the Church as against those of the lay world.   The

aggrandisement of the Papacy was also an object with him, and, although it can no longer be contended that this was his primary or sole object, it tended to be one of the effects, nor was Nicholas I. slow to avail himself of the power it supplied. To make the epis-copate a caste apart from the laity, safe from lay accusations or lay tribunals, was an obvious desire of the writer ; and thus Pope Eusebius is made to say : " It has hitherto been observed and ruled that the laity should not accuse the bishops, because they are not of the same mode of life "; the carnal and the spiritual having nothing in common. And so Pope Felix is made to write : " It has been decreed by the rules of the synods that no one should accuse a bishop before secular judges ". Another solicitude of the writer on behalf of the bishops was to protect them from the tyranny of their metropolitans and to confirm their right of appeal to Rome.

In the chaotic state of the world in the ninth cen-tury after the death of Charlemagne there was much excuse for a writer's identifying the cause of the Church with the maintenance of order ; and in trying to strengthen his case by inventing for Popes letters which they never wrote, he did not always exceed the claims of previous centuries on behalf of the Church. A claim for the actual divinity of bishops went back at least to the time of Constantine, for Rufinus in his history (1-2) thus tells the story of the emperor's address to the bishops he had collected for the Nicene Council : " God hath made you priests and given you the power of sitting in judgment even over us. And therefore we are rightly judged by you, but you cannot be judged by men. Wherefore as between one another look for judgment from God alone, that whatever disputes you may have may be reserved for that Divine trial; for you have been given to us as gods by God (*nobis a Deo dati estis dii*). It is not fitting that a man should judge gods, save Him alone of whom it is written 'God standeth in the congregation of the gods : He judgeth among the gods' (*Deus stetit in synagoga deorum, in medio autem deos discernit*)" (Ps. lxxxii. 1).

The claim for episcopacy could hardly go beyond this, from which of course flowed as a corollary that right of the Church to absolute independence of the State on which the writer of the "False Decretals" was so insistent. Church and State were related as Spiritual and Carnal, between which it was held there could be no communion.

These exalted claims for the Church and the Papacy were not so much invented by the writer as stereotyped by him and successfully imposed by him on the world for many centuries. This is specially true of the "Donation of Constantine," which was incorporated in his second part by the writer, but which had been composed in the preceding century by some unknown Roman ecclesiastic. It was first mentioned in 777 by Pope Hadrian I., and Dollinger's theory seems a plausible one, that its inventor's aim was to bring the whole of Italy into one kingdom ruled by the Pope, and so to free it from the divided control of the Lombards and Greeks.

In the history of the Church there were many other forged "Donations" besides that of Constantine; there was, for instance, King Pepin's Donation of nearly the whole of Italy to the Pope; but all such attempts sink into insignificance by the side of the "Donation of Constantine," which, consisting as it does of only a few pages, has probably had more influence on the course of human history than anything else of human invention.

It purports to be addressed by the emperor, with all his titles, to Pope Sylvester and all his successors who shall sit in the seat of the Blessed Peter to the end of time. Constantine begins with a full profession of the Christian faith as he had been taught it by Sylvester, who had turned him from idols and all the pomps of Satan to the true faith. And then follows the interesting story of this conversion : how, when his whole flesh was a mass of leprosy, and many physicians proved unavailing, the priests of the Capitol bade the emperor wash in water filled with the blood of little children ; but how Constantine, pitying the weeping mothers, ordered their children to be restored to them, and would have no resort to so cruel a remedy. That same night St. Peter and St. Paul stood before him, and bade him send for Sylvester, then a fugitive with his clergy in the caves of Mount Soracte; he would baptise him three times, and all his leprosy would be healed. In return Con-

stantine was to order the restoration of all churches
throughout the world, and himself to forsake idols,
and worship the true God.   Next day Constantine
sent for Sylvester, and, having asked to see pictures
of St. Peter and St. Paul, confessed with a great
shout before all his courtiers that these were identical
with the figures he had seen in his sleep.   Then
Sylvester prescribed a course of penance in the
Lateran Palace; the emperor confessed his belief
in Christianity before all the people, and the ceremony of baptism washed away his leprosy.

Such an incident could not but make the emperor
both grateful and generous, and Constantine's generosity knew no bounds.   The Imperial power and
dignity of Rome he transferred forthwith to the
Roman Church, which was henceforth to be supreme
not only over the churches of Alexandria, Antioch,
Jerusalem, Constantinople, but over all other churches
in the world.   And the Pope was to be supreme over
all other priests in the world, and to be the disposer of
all things that touched worship or faith.   And the
church which Constantine had built on the Lateran
was to be called and reverenced as the head of all
the churches of the world; whilst on the Blessed
Saints Peter and Paul and on the Pope and his successors for ever was conferred the Lateran Palace itself, finer than all others on earth, together with the
Imperial diadem ("the crown of our head") and in
general all the robes, sceptres and ornaments of the
Imperial dignity.

As the Pope was to take the place of the emperor, so were the priests of the Church to take the place of the ancient civil power ; the powers and privileges of the senate and consuls of Rome were to pass to them ; the Roman clergy were to wear the senatorial white sandals, and to ride on horses with white coverings.

But even this surrender was not complete nor abject enough. With his own hands the emperor placed on Sylvester's head that mitre or white Phrygian cap that symbolised the Resurrection, and held the bridle of his horse. Moreover, he gave up to him the Lateran Palace, and all the provinces, places and cities of Rome and Italy, or the western regions (" Romanæ et omnes Italiæ seu occidentalium regionum provincias, loca, et civitates . . . nostro Silvestro universali papæ concedimus atque relinquimus ").

And, since it was not fitting that where the head of the Christian religion reigned an earthly emperor should hold dominion, to the city called after him in the East would Constantine transfer his rule. And his successors for all time he bound by the most solemn vows never to infringe on these concessions.

It is difficult to conceive a bolder or more glorious fiction, or one more successful. It held the credulity of the world throughout the middle ages, and to this day influences the mode of thought of many millions. No one seems to have inquired whether as a fact the emperors after Constantine had given up the rule of the West, or to have remembered that Constantine was really baptised by the Arian Bishop Eusebius at Nicomedia shortly before his death, not at his conversion, nor in Rome at all.

Both the " Donation " and the " Decretals " had an incalculable effect upon history, and in some directions a good effect. Nicholas I., one of the greatest of the Popes (858-867), made use of the " Decretals " in his successful interposition for the protection of Rothad, Bishop of Soissons, against the arbitrary oppression of Hincmar, Archbishop of Rheims. Hincmar had deposed and imprisoned Rothad with the aid of Charles the Bald (862). Nicholas demanded his restoration from Charles, and, having summoned Rothad to Rome, reinstated him and sent him back to his see in France, Hincmar pleading in vain the inapplicability of the " Decretals " to France. There can be little doubt but that in this direction of protecting the bishops and clergy against the tyranny of metropolitans and the secular powers the " Decretals " had a beneficial effect by strengthening the hands of the Popes.

But the greatest effect flowed from the territorial concession to the Papacy. The writer's words only applied to Rome and Italy *or* the western regions. The word "seu" for "or" was intended as explanatory : "Italy, that is the western regions," meaning Istria, Corsica and Sardinia, not such countries as France, Spain, Britain, which in Constantine's time belonged to the Roman dominion. So it was long understood, but in course of time the more extensive claim was made, and Anselm of Lucca, in referring to the " Donation," substituted the word " and " for the more ambiguous " or ".   Constantine, according to him, conceded the Imperial power in Rome and Italy "and in the western parts ".   This would have made most kingdoms of Europe mere fiefs of the Papacy.

A notion arose that Constantine had specially conferred all islands on the Papacy, albeit there is no reference to islands in the document.   It was thus in virtue of the " Donation " that the English Pope, Hadrian IV., claimed the possession of Ireland, and then conferred it on Henry II. (1155) as, like all Christian islands, belonging of right to St. Peter and the Roman Church.   Hadrian's friend, John of Salisbury, who persuaded him to this step, refers to the " Donation " as the ground of this grant ; and thus began that long struggle between England and Ireland which has proved so disastrous for both countries.   In all other gifts of newly discovered islands or continents the Papacy was but disposing of territories which Constantine had implicitly bestowed upon itself.

Pope Nicholas I., during whose Pontificate the " False Decretals " appeared, undoubtedly made use of them for the extension of the papal power ; but it was not till about two centuries later that they became effective for that establishment of a pure theocracy over the world at which the papal party then definitely aimed.   With the Pontificate of Gregory VII., in the eleventh century, a new storey of the ecclesiastical edifice was raised, and the forgery of Isidore was utilised and improved upon by Anselm of Lucca, who composed about 1083 a new collection of Church law.   The names of Cardinal Deusdedit, Cardinal Gregory of Pavia, and Bonizo, are those of other diligent and successful workers in the same school.   The power to dethrone kings and emperors was now boldly formulated, and the supremacy of the Canon law over all civil laws or institutions.   If in an earlier age the bishops had claimed to be gods, a slight alteration in the story of Constantine and the bishops at Nicea enabled the Pope to claim divinity :—

"It is clearly enough shown that the Pope cannot be bound or loosed by the secular power, seeing that it is agreed that he was by the pious Prince Constantine called a God, and it is manifest that a God cannot be judged by men" (Gratian's *Dist.*, 96, 7).

After this it is not surprising to find the Canonists claiming for all decretals of the Popes (including Isidore's) a place among the Canonical Scriptures. "Among the Canonical Scriptures the decretal epistles are counted," said Gratian, who but borrowed from Anselm and Cardinal Gregory a wilful falsification of a passage in St. Augustine.   Gratian's famous "Decretum," appearing at Bologna about the year 1150, and displacing all the older collections of the Canon law, added fresh fabrications to those it incorporated from Isidore, Anselm, and the others.   The right or duty of the Church to constrain men to faith by torture, and to execute and confiscate the property of heretics was elaborated by Gratian in a number of canons. No book had an influence equal to Gratian's on the history of the Church, and therefore of the world. Now was firmly established the right of the Pope to dispense as he pleased even with all laws of the Church, thus rendering him an absolutely arbitrary autocrat. And on Gratian was built all the ecclesiastical jurisprudence of the middle ages.

But ecclesiastical forgery never ceased. Dominican writers themselves confess that St. Thomas of Aquinas had been deceived by a forgery when he relied on certain passages of the Greek fathers, more especially of Cyril of Alexandria, to introduce into dogmatic theology the doctrine of the infallibility and absolute power of the Pope; and that St. Thomas, himself deceived, deceived a long succession of subsequent theologians and canonists. And to the same end served many a history of the Church, deliberately falsified. When one considers all that flowed from this systematic fraud, all the struggles between Popes and secular rulers, the depositions of kings and emperors, the excommunications, the inquisitions, indulgences, absolutions, persecutions and burnings, and reflects that all this miserable history was the direct product of a series of forgeries of which the " Donation of Constantine " and the " False Decretals " were not indeed the earliest, but the most important, one is disposed to wonder whether falsehood rather than truth has not had the more permanent effect on the destinies of mankind.

But the light of truth penetrated at last even this egregious edifice of fiction. In the fifteenth century criticism effectually pierced the thick mass of deceit, and exposed the spuriousness of the " Decretals," the " Donation," and of much besides. To Cardinal Nicholas de Cusa and Laurentius Valla belongs the honour of first establishing the truth ; and remarkable it is that, despite the damaging blows dealt by Valla's treatise at the papal system, he was taken into the service of Nicholas V. after its appearance, and received both from him and his successor, Calixtus III., signal marks of their favour.

Nor in this honourable rivalry must Reginald Pococke, for a brief spell Bishop of Chichester, be forgotten, who about 1449 published that enlightened work against the Lollards, called the *Repression of Overmuch Blaming of the Clergy*, which with other books of his he was not only compelled to recant but to burn with his own hands at St. Paul's Cross a few years later. The attempt to vindicate the genuineness of the "Decretals" by the Jesuit Torres in 1572 led to its more total discomfiture at the hands of the Calvinist divine David Blondel in 1628. And now it only remains as the greatest monument of successful imposture that the world can show or that the genius of man has ever produced ; the strongest chain for the enslavement of the human spirit that the Catholic priestcraft ever succeeded in forging.

CHAPTER VIII.

THE TRAGEDY OF CHATTERTON.

THE name of Chatterton has supplied the English
language with a synonym for a literary forger, and
the controversy is long since dead which raged so
fiercely round the authenticity of the poems which
Chatterton at the age of sixteen copied, as he alleged,
from the poems of Thomas Rowley, the monk of the
fifteenth century, taken by Chatterton's father from the
old chest at St. Mary Redcliffe's Church at Bristol.
It was finally laid to rest by Professor Skeat's Essay
on the Rowley poems prefixed to the second volume
of his edition of Chatterton's *Poetical Works* (1871).
The youthful poet himself supplied the verses, and
then proceeded by the help of Kersey's or Bailey's
Dictionaries of Anglo-Saxon to give them an air of
antiquity. But this plan involved the poet in the
mistakes of his authorities, as where we find him using
the word " cherisaunei," not " cherisaunce," for *com-
fort*, owing to Kersey having preceded him in that
identical error.

But when stripped of their garb of pseudo-anti-
quity and transposed into modern and legible English,
as they are in Professor Skeat's edition, the Rowley

poems are remarkable works, whose production should have entitled Chatterton's memory to more lenient treatment than it ever received. Here was a poor youth, after such education as he might have received as a Blue-coat schoolboy, immured at the age of fourteen in a lawyer's office for twelve hours a day, living with a widowed mother and sister in indigent circumstances; yet at the age of sixteen and seventeen he is capable of writing poems from which even those of his contemporaries who were most condemnatory of the deception could not withhold their admiration. Malone, whose *Cursory Observations* on the Rowley poems (1782) contributed so much to discredit them, pronounced Chatterton to be, in his opinion, the greatest genius that England had produced since the days of Shakespeare, whilst Walpole expressed the opinion, which occurs to all who come fresh to the study of the poems, that almost more of a miracle was involved in their being written by a youth of Chatterton's age than in all the difficulties of metre and diction involved in their ascription to Rowley. The choice of subjects, the felicity of phrase and metaphors, the harmony of rhythm, displayed in such poems as the " Bristowe Tragedie," " Ælla," or the " Battle of Hastings," would have conferred credit on any poet, whilst they are entirely free from any of those marks of immaturity which alone might have been expected to betray the boyhood of their real composer.

It was this consideration which convinced Chatter-

ton's friend Thistlethwaite of the reality of Rowley
and his poems.   Chatterton, he argued, would
never, with his thirst for praise, have ascribed to
another what was calculated to confer so much
honour on himself.   Nor has this point been ever
cleared up by the vast army of Chatterton's bio-
graphers.   What set him to write verse in the name
of Rowley and other imaginary mediæval poets, if
he were himself capable of writing verse worthy of
receiving recognition?   There must have been more
design in it than the mere dreamy pleasure of living
poetically in a bygone age.

That design was probably nothing more than to
use the acquired reputation of Rowley as a stepping-
stone to his own personal recognition as an aspirant
to poetical rank.   Had his design not miscarried,
Rowley, having served his purpose, would probably
have been disavowed, and the truth acknowledged.
In such a course he would have perhaps appealed to
the case of the precedent set him by Horace Walpole
in his *Castle of Otranto.*   The first edition of this
appeared in 1764, when Chatterton was twelve, and
was ushered into the world by Walpole under the
following preface, which, if not intended, was at least
calculated to deceive many :—

"The following work was found in the library of
an ancient Catholic family in the north of England.
It was printed at Naples, in the black-letter, in the
year 1529.   How much sooner it was written does
not appear. . . . The style is the purest Italian.

10 *

If the story was written near the time when it is
supposed to have happened, it must have been
between 1095, the era of the first crusade, and 1243,
the date of the last or not long afterwards. . . . It
is natural for a translator to be prejudiced in favour
of his adopted work. . . . Should it meet with the
success I hope for, I may be encouraged to reprint
the original Italian, though it will tend to depreciate
my own labour," etc.

Every word of this of course was false, but the
falsehood proved a successful advertisement, and in
his preface to the second edition in 1766 the author
offered the following cavalier apology to the public
he had trifled with :—

" It is fit that he should ask pardon of his readers
for having offered his work to them under the borrowed personage of a translator. As diffidence of
his own abilities, and the novelty of the attempt, were
the sole inducements to assume that disguise, he
flatters himself he shall appear excusable."

Had Chatterton once succeeded in getting his
antique poems published, might he not as reason-
ably as Walpole have asked pardon of his readers for
having offered his work to them under the borrowed
personage of a transcriber? That fatal dose of
arsenic or opium before he was quite eighteen leaves
us to pure surmise about Chatterton's real design.
But had the poems been once published as antiques,
would their publication under such false colours have
been divided by any impassable moral gulf from the

publication of the *Castle of Otranto* under the fictions prefixed to it by Horace Walpole?

With this theory of Chatterton's probable design, to which Walpole's successful example possibly contributed, the facts of his story completely coincide. The first step being to get his compositions published, he must perforce seek for a publisher for " Ælla " and some others of his poems. Therefore the first attempt was on Dodsley, the publisher, whose curiosity he tried to arouse by an offer to send him copies of " several ancient poems, and an interlude, perhaps the oldest dramatic piece extant, wrote by one Rowley, a priest of Bristol, who lived in the reigns of Henry VI. and Edward IV." (21st December, 1768). Then two months later (15th February, 1769) came another attempt ; the possessor of the tragedy of " Ælla," of which he had obtained a sight after a long search, would not part with it for less than a guinea. The publisher should have a copy for that sum, though the writer had no mercenary views, and, were he able, would print it at his own risk. If the publisher would give him an estimate of the expense of such printing, he would try to publish it by subscription on his own account.

When the publisher proved as deaf as is the wont of his kind to these siren suggestions, Chatterton must turn elsewhere ; and to whom could he better turn for help and patronage than to that very Horace Walpole whose publication of the *Castle of Otranto* seemed to hold out, in case of need, some

promise of sympathy and assistance? So with him
he began a correspondence (25th March, 1769) with
deliberate attempt to deceive. It was this attempt
that widely differentiated the Rowley poems morally
from the more conventional deception of the *Castle
of Otranto*. Walpole replied on the 28th in a letter
of almost fulsome politeness, declaring that the verses
sent him as a specimen of the Abbot John's of the
twelfth century were "wonderful for their harmony
and spirit"; accepting Chatterton's assertion that
the said Abbot had invented oil-painting in England
at a date anterior to its discovery by John Ab Eyck;
asking where Rowley's poems were to be found, and
adding the welcome intelligence that he should "not
be sorry to print them, or at least a specimen of
them," if they had never been printed.

Chatterton must have felt that he had indeed
"struck oil," and at the very first attempt. Forthwith more specimens of antiquity were posted to
Walpole with some account of the writer's circumstances. But this time the specimens were suspected,
Walpole's own scepticism being confirmed by that of
the poets Mason and Gray, who at once pronounced
them forgeries. Walpole intimated as much to
Chatterton, and added the sensible advice that the
poet should stick to his profession as a lawyer till the
attainment of a sufficient fortune justified his indulgence
in literary studies. Chatterton's reply (8th April)
proves that the kindness of Walpole's advice nearly
prevailed: he could not dispute with Walpole; he

had copied Rowley's poems from a copy in the possession of a gentleman who was assured of their authenticity and had long possessed them. Though only sixteen, he could see that poverty was the lot of literature. He was obliged for Walpole's advice, and would go a little beyond it, by destroying all his "useless lumber of literature" and never using his pen in future but in the law.

There seems no reason to doubt Chatterton's sincerity in this letter. Well for him had it been, had he kept to his first impulse, and accepted the older man's advice. In the letter of self-vindication written by Walpole in 1778, he was justified in saying that his letter to Chatterton had been written "with as much kindness and tenderness as if he had been his guardian". Considering that Walpole was then aware that his unknown and youthful correspondent had tried to make him his dupe, the letter of paternal advice might well have been one of indignant remonstrance. And if Chatterton had calculated that Walpole would have a fellow-feeling for him, even if he detected the fraud, his calculation was not erroneous, for Walpole expressly says that he deemed it "no grave crime in a young bard to have forged false notes of hand that were to pass current only in the parish of Parnassus". It was only what he had himself done in the matter of his *Castle of Otranto*.

So far all was well. Walpole's moral sense had taken no offence at the attempted imposition, though abundance of that came later, when Walpole's own

conduct in connection with Chatterton had come to
be impugned. But then came the breach. Within
a week Chatterton wrote again to Walpole, asking
politely for the return of the Rowley papers, of whose
genuineness he was "fully convinced," and adding in
a postscript: "If you will publish them yourself,
they are at your service" (14th April). This extraordinary suggestion, and evident hope, that Walpole
would himself publish poems of whose spuriousness
he had already expressed no uncertain opinion, seems
to prove that in addressing himself to Walpole rather
than to any other literary man of the time, Chatterton felt that the merit of the works submitted to
Walpole's judgment would override considerations of
the truth about their authorship. It might have
been so, had not Walpole, then just departing for
Paris, forgotten to return the copies; thereby exposing himself to an angry letter from Chatterton on
his return (dated 24th July), complaining of his
inattention to a repeated request for the return of
the papers. These were returned on the 4th of
August; but there was an end to all hope of publication through Walpole. The irritation of the boy was
only too natural, nothing being more maddening to
the "irritable race" than the retention of their MSS.,
but it was playing a fatally false card to display it.
Walpole, more judiciously treated, might still have
assisted.

In later years Walpole attributed to the success
of the Ossian poems, of which he himself had been

at first a dupe, Chatterton's idea of the Rowley poems ; but such success had not been achieved by Macpherson when Chatterton in his early boyhood composed his ballad of " Elinoure and Juga ". This cannot have been the specimen of Rowley which he sent to Walpole, for he published it in the *Town and Country Magazine* for May, 1769, during the very time when Walpole was in possession of the unreturned MSS. After that Chatterton seems to have desisted from his idea of winning fame by poems in the antique style, and to have turned his attention to ordinary composition. Between the August of 1769, when Walpole returned his MSS., and the August of the next year, when he committed suicide, there is not only no more production of ancient poems but little discernible attempt to turn previous productions of that sort to profitable use. This alone would seem to indicate that Walpole, as the author of the *Castle of Otranto*, was approached by Chatterton as alone likely to assist his rise under the personation of Rowley ; for otherwise there were numberless other men of letters to whom he might have applied when Walpole failed. Hence the bitterness which expressed itself against Walpole in the following verses written about this time :—

> Walpole, I thought not I should ever see
> So mean a heart as thine has proved to be.
> Thou who, in luxury nurst, behold'st with scorn
> The boy, who friendless, fatherless, forlorn,
> Asks thy high favour—thou mayst call me cheat—
> Say, didst thou never practise such deceit ?

Who wrote *Otranto*, but I will not chide;
Scorn I'll repay with scorn, and pride with pride.

.　　.　　.　　.　　.　　.　　.　　.　　.

Had I the gifts of wealth and luxury shared,
Not poor and mean, Walpole, thou hadst not dared
Thus to insult.　But I shall live and stand
By Rowley's side, when thou art dead and damned.

These lines lend strong support to the theory of
the close dependence of the Rowley poems on the
Castle of Otranto.　Walpole had won notice for his
work by a false account of its origin; why should
not he, Chatterton, do the same?　And perhaps,
having thus achieved a literary success, proclaim the
truth?　If it were deceit, it was at least deceit
sanctioned by the authority of one of the most
fashionable writers of the day; a legitimate literary
expedient consonant with the highest precedents.
The gentleman therefore who had set the precedent
was naturally the patron to whom to turn.

It was perhaps some consciousness that this was
Chatterton's line of reasoning which led to Walpole's
extreme bitterness against his memory in later years.
For was there not a literary affinity between himself
and the dead poet; and were not the Rowley poems
the direct offspring of the *Castle of Otranto*?　The
appeal to himself to publish poems whose spuriousness he had detected was a clear, though tacit, invitation to repeat on the public the experiment of his
own romance; and the resentment felt at such an
invitation, with all that it implied, was calculated to
increase rather than to diminish with time.　The

obvious way to dissociate his own character from
that of his imitator, and to disavow the discreditable
connexion, was to throw scorn on Chatterton's
memory, and to speak and write of him as a dis-
reputable impostor.   This was the course that Walpole took, and in this he has had many followers.
But posterity can afford to judge of Chatterton more
charitably, and to doubt if he intended a permanent
deception.

Few curiosities in the British Museum are of
more interest than the two thin volumes which contain Chatterton's manuscripts (Add. MSS., 5766, A-
B), and reveal the extreme beauty of his natural
handwriting.

This collection, revealing as it does the fabrication of many of those antique originals of which
Chatterton seldom suffered his contemporaries to
obtain a glimpse, has long since terminated a controversy which was once acute.   But how much of that
controversy was unnecessary!   Take, for instance,
the first part of the " Battle of Hastings ".   It is said
that Chatterton under pressure of his patron Barrett,
the surgeon and the historian of Bristol, confessed
himself the author of this part, but that Barrett refused to believe him.   It is difficult to see why
Barrett should wish to extort a confession he was
predetermined not to believe ; but it is more surprising that he should have wanted a confession at all.
For the copy brought to him by Chatterton bore the
following title : " Battle of Hastings, wrote by

Turgot the Monk, a Saxon, in the tenth century, and translated by Thomas Rowlie, parish preeste of St. Johns in the city of Bristol in the year 1465. The remainder of the poem I have not been happy enough to meet with." But how could Turgot the monk have written a poem in the *tenth* century about a battle which took place in the *eleventh*? How did this common mistake in naming the century come to escape the notice of Barrett and of the many subsequent critics of Chatterton?

There is one point, unnoticed hitherto, which seems clearly to reveal the hand of Chatterton in the longer poems of Rowley. It is undisputed that the so-called translations from the Saxon which Chatterton contributed to the *Town and Country Magazine*, in imitation or ridicule of the Ossianic poems, were his own original compositions: "Whenever asked for the original of these pieces," said his friend Thistlethwaite, " he hesitated not to confess that they existed only in his own imagination, and were merely the offspring and invention of fancy ". One of the main characteristics of these pieces, such as Ethelgar, Kenrick, Cerdick, and others, is the constant reference to wolves, or metaphors drawn from wolves; the wolf in these imaginary translations appears at least twenty-five times, and gives a distinct colouring to all the compositions. But precisely the same characteristic appears both in " Ælla " and in the "Battle of Hastings"; the wolf figuring seven times in " Ælla " and nine times in the " Battle of Hastings"; once in the " Unknown

Knight" : "bold as a mountain wolf he stood". It is
as if Chatterton could not get the wolf off his mind,
or used it purposely to cover his work with the atmosphere of a distant antiquity.

In fairness to Chatterton it should be borne in
mind that he never published the Rowley poems as a
whole. They were not so published till seven years
after his death from such papers as he had given or
sold to George Catcott, the pewterer, and Barrett, the
surgeon, supplemented by what Catcott bought of
Chatterton's mother after her son's death for a paltry
five guineas. Nor was it till after Dean Milles' edition of them in 1782 that the controversy burst into
blaze. It is indeed remarkable that, whilst in 1769
Chatterton published his six Saxon works in the *Town
and Country Magazine*, the " Elinoure and Juga" is
the only Rowley poem which he published in it.
The " Balade of Charitie" was offered to the editor
of that magazine shortly before Chatterton's death,
but it was rejected, and during the last four months
of his life spent in London, whither he had started
from Bristol with so much hope, and where he was
destined to die in such unaccountable and unexplained
despair, there was little serious attempt, and no successful attempt, to turn the Rowley poems into money.
Poems and political writings of his own amply occupied his time, nor is it possible to judge to what
extent, in a future that never came, he might have
tried to deceive the public with the Rowley poems.
That he deceived Catcott, and Barrett at Bristol,

and was wishful to deceive Dodsley and Walpole in London cannot be gainsaid ; but whether he intended to carry such deception farther than its use as a means of introduction to a powerful and literary patron cannot now be determined.

It is difficult to conceive of any other motive ; for there was no reward to be expected from such patrons as Catcott and Barrett that could have at all compensated for the labour involved in his compositions. And when all is said that can be said about their faults, their anachronisms, or their plagiarisms, they must ever remain among the marvels as well as the puzzles of literature. Dean Milles, Mr. Bryant, and other believers in their authenticity, had considerable material as well as moral basis for their belief. For it was beyond doubt that the chest at St. Mary Redcliffe's had been forced open in the time of Chatterton's father ; that the father had been one of the main spoilers of its documentary contents ; that he had used some of these for covering children's copy-books, and kept many others stored in a box ; that the son carried these parchments with him to Mr. Lambert's office, where out of twelve nominal hours of work he often had ten at his own disposal. It rested on the fair contemporary evidence of eye-witnesses that he was often found at the office copying some ancient documents: Thistlethwaite in 1768 "at divers visits" found him "employed in copying Rowley" from what he always considered "authentic and undoubted originals" ; whilst Smith vouched for Chatterton's having often read to him whole treatises or parts of poems from ancient MSS., of which he had seen a dozen and which he had often seen Chatterton transcribe at the office. This office was described as strewn with piles of such documents. No one will ever know now what these documents were, or whether those which Chatterton copied corresponded with the works which he produced as ancient writings. But it is impossible to get over the evidence that there was this solid basis of fact both for Chatterton's story and for the belief of those who accepted it. It may be that Chatterton's idea was to utilise these old documents as materials for the acquisition of the old style and phraseology, and that he furthered his plan by pretending to his friends that they were the originals of his fabrications. In that case his stratagem was singularly successful.

Chatterton's fabrications in prose are even more marvellous than those he produced in verse. It is difficult to conceive of any imagination elaborating the details about the antiquities of churches with which he provided Barrett for his history of Bristol. And the same must be said of his Inscriptions, Proclamations and Deeds. Whether or not the Thomas Rowle, whom the registers of Wells prove to have been made an acolyte in 1439 (Bryant's *Observations*, 536, 544), was the individual of Chatterton's Rowley, the youthful poet has endowed his fifteenth-century monk with a semblance of life which can never cease to astonish the readers of his works, and which has

given to him a more real existence than many past
actual lives now enjoy.

There is no evidence to justify the black colours
in which Chatterton's general character has by some
writers been painted. And there is abundant evidence to prove a character possessed of many laud-
able virtues. Against his vanity and resort to deceit
must be set his indefatigable industry, so that after
twelve hours' confinement in Mr. Lambert's office
he would often, says his sister, "sit up all night and
write by moonlight". The affection and generosity
he always showed to his mother and sister are also
among the more pleasing aspects of his character.
In which connexion a singular pathos attaches to
the last, though far from the best, verses he ever
wrote, which bear the date of 24th August, 1770,
the day of his death :—

> Farewell, Bristolia's dingy piles of brick,
> Lovers of Mammon, worshippers of Trick!
> Ye spurned the boy who gave you antique lays,
> And paid for learning with your empty praise.
> Farewell, ye guzzling aldermanic fools,
> By nature fitted for Corruption's tools!
> I go to where celestial anthems swell;
> But you, when you depart, will sink to hell.
> Farewell, my mother! cease, my anguished soul,
> Nor let Distraction's billows o'er me roll!
> Have mercy, Heaven! when here I cease to live,
> And this last act of wretchedness forgive.

CHAPTER IX.

THE SHAME OF LAUDER.

OF all the stories of literary forgery none is more remarkable than that connected with the name of William Lauder, one of the foremost scholars of the eighteenth century. Few men of his time could write better Latin than this Scotch schoolmaster, a graduate of Edinburgh University, or were more widely versed in ancient and modern literature. Yet he succumbed to a miserable temptation in his passion to prove that Milton in writing *Paradise Lost* was merely a plagiarist from previous authors.

Lauder, in his zeal to prove his point, could not content himself with adducing passages from Grotius, Massenius, and others, which it would have been fair to contend that Milton might, or must, have seen, or even copied; to make the resemblances more striking he imported into the quoted passages either lines of his own composition or even lines from the Latin translation by Hog of Milton himself. As a sample of this latter method let one glaring instance suffice. Milton thus describes one of the consequences of Adam's fall :—

> Beast now with beast 'gan war, and fowl with fowl,
> And fish with fish; to graze the herb all leaving
> Devoured each other : nor stood much in awe
> Of man, but fled him, or with countenance grim
> Glared on him passing. (x, 710.)

Lauder took the following translation of these lines from Hog's Latin version of *Paradise Lost ;* incorporated them in a passage of the *Sarcotis* of Massenius; and then declared this translation of Milton to have been the source of Milton's own passage !—

> Quadrupedi pugnat quadrupes, volucrique volucris,
> Et piscis cum pisce ferox hostilibus armis
> Proelia sæva gerit ; jam pristina pabula spernunt
> Jam tondere piget viridantes gramine campos,
> Alterum et alterius vivunt animalia letho,
> Prisca nec in gentem humanam reverentia durat,
> Sed fugiunt vel si steterant, fera bella minantur
> Fronte truci torvosque oculos jaculantur in illum.

Lauder must have relied on two things : the improbability of any one procuring a copy of the Jesuit's poem, and the still greater improbability of any one's referring to so little known a work as Hog's translation.   But he reckoned without the Rev. John Douglas, afterwards Bishop of Salisbury, whose suspicions, leading to a search in Hogæus, were promptly found to be justified.   In a letter to the Earl of Bath in 1750 Douglas published his *Milton Vindicated from the Charge of Plagiarism*, and triumphantly exposed to the world the base devices to which Lauder had resorted.

The reason for Lauder's hostility to Milton was

hardly less extraordinary than his method of displaying it.   The famous Scotch writer George
Buchanan, who played so conspicuous a part in the
politics of the time of Mary Queen of Scots, had when
travelling in Portugal in early life fallen into the
hands of the Inquisition and been shut up in a
prison.   As a pastime or as a condition of his libera-
tion he there composed in different Latin metres
that admirable paraphrase of the Hebrew Psalms
which was destined to assist the education of so
many generations of Scotchmen.   In the following
century Arthur Johnston, for some time physician to
Charles I., published a no less admirable translation
of the Psalms in Latin elegiacs ; and it occurred to
Lauder with much reason that Johnston's translation
would be better adapted for the lower classes in the
Scotch grammar schools than the more difficult
version of Buchanan.   Accordingly he published an
edition of Johnston for that purpose, and petitioned
the General Assembly of the Kirk of Scotland to
recommend its use to the schools.   He did not suggest its adoption to the exclusion of Buchanan, but
only its use as a stepping-stone to the " full and perfect understanding of Buchanan's more masterly and
sublime but more difficult paraphrase ".   The Assembly complied with his request, recommending the
use of Buchanan for the higher classes and the
universities (30th November, 1740).   About the
same time William Benson, also an admirer of
Johnston, published some fine editions of his Psalms,

11 *

and defended their Latinity as superior to that of Buchanan.

A bitter literary war ensued in Scotland between the rival partisans of Buchanan and of Johnston, in the course of which Lauder wrote to Pope for his judgment on the greater fitness of Johnston than of Buchanan for the use of juvenile classes. The poet vouchsafed no answer, but in the *Dunciad* held up both Benson and Johnston to undeserved ridicule :—

> On two unequal crutches propped he (Benson) came,
> Milton on this, on that one Johnston's name.

The slighting way in which Benson's patronage of Johnston was thus compared with his admiration of Milton proved fatal to Lauder's hope of ever getting his edition of Johnston into the schools. "From this time all my praises of Johnston became ridiculous, and I was censured with great freedom for forcing upon the schools an author whom Mr. Pope had mentioned only as a foil to a better poet. On this occasion it was natural not to be pleased, and my resentment seeking to discharge itself somewhere was unhappily directed against Milton. I resolved to attack his fame."

These words occur in Lauder's humble confession to John Douglas (29th December, 1750), and they constituted his first line of defence, from which his second one of a few years later differed considerably. He asserted the same fact of Pope's influence in a letter of apology addressed to the Archbishop of

Canterbury in 1751 : " Such was the blind deference to Mr. Pope that few schoolmasters in Scotland would receive Johnston's paraphrase into their schools after that capricious critic testified his dislike of that performance by the slighting manner in which he treated its author in comparison of Milton, whom he treated as a giant in poetry and the other as a dwarf or pigmy only ".

This meant for Lauder an annual loss of some £20 or £30 a year, a serious inroad on the scanty resources of a teacher of humanity at Edinburgh in those days. Lauder, despite his unquestioned abilities, had been dogged all his life by failure. He had failed in his candidature both for the post of Professor of Humanity in Edinburgh (1734) and for the post of University Librarian. And he failed to obtain the rectorship of the grammar school at Dundee the very same year (1742) in which Pope deprived him of all hope of an income from Johnston. There was nothing for it but to leave Scotland an embittered man, and to try in London to eke out such a livelihood as private tuition and his pen might afford him.

Regarding Milton as the source of his woes he devoted a large portion of the next four years to collecting materials for his attack on the fame of the poet, the result appearing in 1747 in the *Gentleman's Magazine* under the title of Zoilus, the bitter Alexandrian critic of Homer. The papers produced an impression. Richard Richardson replied to Lauder in a pamphlet entitled *Zoilomastix*, but his criticism went no farther than challenging the force of the compared passages; he had no suspicion of the aid derived from forgery. Dr. Newton in his edition of *Paradise Lost*, published in 1749, inserted in his notes several of the parallelisms from Grotius' *Adamus Exul*, which were afterwards acknowledged to have been forged.

Towards the end of 1749 Lauder republished the papers as a whole under the title of *An Essay on Milton's Use and Imitation of the Moderns in his "Paradise Lost"*. Might not the fraud continue undetected? Warburton wrote at the time (23rd December, 1749): "I have just read the most silly and knavish book I ever saw, one Lauder on Milton's imitations. . . . In one view the book does not displease me. It is likely enough to mortify all the silly adorers of Milton who deserve to be laughed at" (Nichols, *Lit. Ill.*, ii., 177). Sir John Hawkins declared that the short preface to the essay, written as if by the author, was (as was also the postscript) "indubitably written by Dr. Johnson," then forty-one, whom he accuses of sympathy with an argument which he hoped might injure Milton's reputation. But Johnson can only be fairly convicted of a natural sympathy with an inquiry of much legitimate interest in itself; when the imposition was discovered, Johnson's indignation was as genuine as that of Lauder's publishers, and it was under his dictation that Lauder wrote that letter of apology to Douglas of which the wonder is that any one could have survived the writing.

But Boswell's remark that Lauder's passages produced from other writers bore only "a faint resemblance to some parts of *Paradise Lost*" somewhat understates the case. Lauder always contended that his case was complete in itself even if "stript of all adventitious assistance," and that the latter was small in amount. But of twelve passages of resemblance cited from Grotius' *Adamus Exul* ten consisted wholly or in part of interpolations of Lauder's own composition! As a sample take Milton's well-known lines :—

And in my choice
To reign is worth ambition, though in Hell,
Better to reign in Hell than serve in Heaven.

Lauder interpolated the following lines into Grotius as their source :—

Nam, me judice,
Regnare dignum est ambitu, etsi in Tartaro,
Alto præesse Tartaro siquidem juvat
Cœli quam in ipsis servi obire munia.

But though Lauder's passages from Grotius were of this type, it remains probable that Milton had been influenced by the tragedy written by Grotius at the age of eighteen. This was the view taken by Mr. F. Barham, who in 1839 published the *Adamus Exul of Grotius, or the Prototype of "Paradise Lost"*. With an original copy of the *Adamus* in his hands he vouched for the general fidelity of Lauder's version. It seems to have been the parent tree (1601) of all later modern works on the same subject ; being more or less imitated by Andreini in his *Paradiso Per-*

duto (1613), by Andrew Ramsay in his *Sacred Poems* (1633), by Massenius in his *Sarcotis* (1650); but, adds Barham, "by none was it so closely followed, so admirably emulated and improved upon as by our Milton".

Subsequent research has considerably enlarged the sources which may either have influenced Milton or have been utilised by him. They are collected in Hayley's *Conjectures on the Origin of "Paradise Lost,"* at the end of his life of Milton (1796). Many of these were unknown to Lauder: such as Marino's *Strage di gli Innocenti* (1633), Serafino della Sallandra's *Adamo Perduto* (1647) and others; but what would Lauder not have given to have known the *Lucifer* of the Dutch poet Vondel, of whose later discovered relation to Milton a modern writer has said: "The very large use which he (Milton) made without acknowledgment of the ideas and language of a distinguished contemporary, from works but recently published and written in a tongue unknown to the vast majority of English readers, cannot be altogether excused or defended"? (Edmundson's *Milton and Vondel*, 191). Undoubtedly Lauder would have used stronger language than Mr. Edmundson. And in any case his shade must look with satisfaction on the tardy but general acceptance of his denial of the absolute originality of Milton, which before his unscrupulous onslaught had been an article of faith in the world of English letters.

Lauder prevailed on the Archbishop of Canter-

bury to forgive him the imposition practised on his
Grace in common with lesser mortals who had assisted the author in the original publication. Under
the archiepiscopal patronage he was suffered to publish his *Delectus auctorum sacrorum Miltono facem
prælucentium*, which contained Andrew Ramsay's
Sacra Poemata in four books of Latin hexameters,
and the *Adamus Exul* of Grotius (1752). But it
was too late then with any chance of success to run a
fresh tilt against Milton.

Time, however, failed to cool his animosity against
the poet who had so unwittingly injured his livelihood. In 1754 he came forward with a fresh charge
against Milton, and at the same time with a fresh
justification of his own frauds. We hear no more in
his *Charles I. Vindicated* (1754) of Pope, nor of
Johnston's Psalms. He now claims to have committed his frauds with the express hope of detection.
For such detection was to have enabled him to bring
with all the greater force a similar charge of forgery
against Milton. Only so could he have effectively
charged Milton with tampering with the publication
of the *Eikon Basilike*, and with interpolating it at
the end with the prayer, as being the king's, which is
borrowed almost verbally from Pamela's prayer in
Sidney's *Arcadia*.

Milton's motive, according to Lauder, was, by
discrediting the royal authorship of the prayers
appended to the *Eikon*, to discredit the royal authorship of the whole work. "As Milton by that im-

posture could easily prove that the king was not the author of this prayer, so he meant that an inference should be drawn that he was not the author of the treatise itself."

For this story of Milton forcing Dugard, the schoolmaster-printer, caught in the act of printing the *Eikon*, to subjoin to it Pamela's prayer, Lauder cites as his authority three letters, two of which were first quoted by T. Wagstaffe in 1697 in his *Vindication of Charles I.*, and subsequently printed by Dr. T. Birch in his Appendix to his *Life of Milton* (1738). But the first edition of Wagstaffe's *Vindication* in 1693 is without the letters, and their late date makes them suspicious. One is a letter from Dr. Gill to Charles Hatton, dated 1st May, 1694, in which Gill, physician for several years to Hills, Cromwell's printer, refers to Hills as telling him how Milton used his influence with Bradshaw to relieve Dugard from further penalty for printing the *Eikon* on condition of his adding to it Pamela's prayer. The other is a letter, which Wagstaffe declared to be in his own possession, from Dr. Francis Bernard, who was also a physician to Hills, and who also heard from him the same story (10th May, 1694). Dr. Birch quotes a third letter from Bernard to Dr. Goodall to the same effect, dated 13th March, 1693, but not derived from Wagstaffe. In his second edition of Milton's *Life* (1753) Dr. Birch withdrew his credit from the story on the ground that it rested only on the hearsay evidence of Hills.

Certain it is that Dugard suffered for printing the *Eikon*, and some other works in the Royalist interest. He was committed to Newgate; his presses were destroyed; he was dismissed from the mastership of the Merchant Taylors' School, and his wife and children were turned out of doors. The fact is attested by the Stationer's Preface to Gauden's *Cromwell's Bloody Slaughter-house* (July, 1660), and by an affidavit by Dugard at the Record Office (October, 1661). But the latter (if it may be trusted) adds the information that it was Sir James Harrington who saved Dugard from being tried for his life; there is no mention of Milton in it at all. This fact alone would seem to discredit the letters against Milton, first published by Wagstaffe, and their appearance at a time, when so much doubtful testimony was eagerly collected in favour of King Charles and of his authorship of the *Eikon*, tends still further to deprive them of value. But Lauder was no more to blame for believing the story than was Dr. Birch in his first edition. Birch in fact was Lauder's authority. The story itself at least gave a plausible account of the presence in the *Eikon* of Pamela's prayer, and no other story has ever been given to account for it. The prayer found no place in the first edition, nor in several of the editions both of 1648 (Old Style) and 1649, but it is present in one edition of 1648, and the question has never been satisfactorily answered how it came to be there.

If we refer to Milton's own language in his

Eikonoclastes about this puzzling prayer, it appears inconceivable that he could have been himself responsible for its presence in the *Eikon*. Let the reader judge for himself whether the poet's indignation, however excessive it may now seem, has not all the stamp of sincerity : " This king," writes Milton, "not content with that which although in a thing holy is no holy theft, to attribute to his own making other men's whole prayers, hath as it were unhallowed and unchristened the very duty of prayer itself by borrowing to a Christian use prayers offered to a heathen god. Who would have imagined so little fear in him of the true all-seeing Deity . . . as immediately before his death to pop into that grave bishop who attended him for a special relique of his saintly exercises a prayer stolen word for word from the mouth of a heathen woman praying to a heathen god ; and that in no serious book but the vain amatorious poem of Sir Philip Sidney's *Arcadia?*" "He whose mind could serve him to seek a Christian prayer out of a pagan legend, and assume it for his own, might gather up the rest God knows where."

Again he alludes to the king's "bankrupt devotion" which "came not honestly by his very prayers, but, having sharked them from the mouth of a heathen worshipper, sold them to those that stood and honoured him next to the Messiah as his own heavenly compositions in adversity, for hopes no less vain and presumptuous than by these goodly relics to be held a saint and martyr with the cheated

people" (from Baron's edition of the *Eikonoclastes*
of 1750, from the second edition of 1650).

In all this there is an evident desire to use
Pamela's prayer as morally discreditable to the
Eikon and its supposed royal author, but there is no
more than a hint of using the prayer as throwing
doubt on the authorship itself. But even so it is not
pleasant to think of Milton, as alleged, foisting this
prayer into the *Eikon* in order to have wherewithal
to lash himself into a fury of righteous indignation
against the lately executed king. One cannot think
it of him, even when allowing for the disturbed state
of public feeling at the time and for a possible desire
to employ any weapon to check the tide of a Royalist
reaction. Yet the question cannot be so disposed
of; it must remain a matter of evidence, of which,
as collected by Lauder, all that can be said is that,
coming from so bitter a source, it is not conclusive.
The presence of the prayer in the *Eikon* must remain an unsolved, and possibly an insoluble, mystery.

In his preface to *Charles I. Vindicated* Lauder
wrote thus of his literary misdemeanour: "Few
men have ever incurred so much infamy and ruin
as I by this rash or if you please unwarrantable zeal
for our abused sovereign". But this must be regarded
as an afterthought, as an attempt to rehabilitate himself in public esteem by an appeal to Royalist sentiment. The attempt was unsuccessful; the public
was deaf to anything further that might be said by
Lauder. From that time he disappeared from the

world's stage. He went finally to the West Indies, where he died in destitute circumstances, and at an advanced age, which cannot be accurately stated; a man of high ability and of wide learning, who wrecked his life to gratify an inordinate passion of literary resentment. There is no case quite like Lauder's in the history of literature, for it is generally against living rather than dead authors that feelings of passionate animosity are aroused. Milton, though dead, was a greater object of hatred to Lauder than were any of his living contemporaries.

CHAPTER X.

THE FORGED LETTERS OF BYRON AND SHELLEY.

It was some time in the summer of 1848 that a young lady called on Mr. White, the bookseller in Pall Mall, and offered him two autograph letters of Lord Byron, which belonged to her elder sister, an invalid, living with her at St. John's Wood. The sister wished to sell them in order to meet a temporary difficulty caused by the defalcation of an agent. The sisters were the daughters of a surgeon, lately dead, who had attended Fletcher, Lord Byron's valet, in his last illness, and from him received certain books which the poet had given as a dying gift to his faithful servant.

The story seeming as plausible as its teller seemed artless and candid, Mr. White bought the letters, and several others at subsequent visits, also by Lord Byron. Then it transpired that the sister had also some letters of Shelley, but with these and the books left by Fletcher to her father she was most reluctant to part. Still if she was compelled to part with them, she would rather they should pass as a whole to Mr. White than that they should be dis-

persed among a number of purchasers.   So Mr.
White gradually became possessed of the whole
collection.

Mr. White speaks of this lady's visits continuing
"over a space of some months," and it is important
to notice, with regard to his part in the story, that
all his dealings with the lady were completed before
the end of the year 1848.   Mr. Sotheby says:
"Very shortly after Mr. White had become possessed
of all the MSS. and letters, the sale of the collection
of autograph letters by the late Mr. Hodges took
place," and 18th December, 1848, was the date of
sale (*Principia Typographica*, ii., 105, 109).   Mr.
White's own narrative clearly represents the whole
transaction as completed before that sale, though
Mr. White makes no mention of its date.

It must have been during the latter months of
1848 that Mr. White acquainted Mr. Murray, the
publisher, with his acquisition of these Byron letters,
and Mr. Moxon, the publisher, with the acquisition
of certain letters by Shelley and Keats.   Mr. Murray,
who had published the seventeen-volume edition
of Lord Byron's letters, journals and life, was naturally interested, and finally there came a day when,
after devoting two hours of study to the forty-seven
Byron letters in the possession of Mr. White, who
would not suffer him to take them to his own house,
Mr. Murray agreed to buy them for the sum of
£123 7s. 6d. ; at the rate, that is, of two and a half
guineas apiece.   The receipt was dated 28th April,

1849. As no one, from his professional connexion with Lord Byron, knew better than Mr. Murray the peculiarities of the handwriting and of the signature of Lord Byron, Mr. Murray's purchase of the letters seemed to Mr. White to settle any possible doubts of their genuineness, and to free him from any necessity of informing Mr. Murray from whom he had acquired them.

No one who has seen these forty-seven letters in the Manuscript Room of the British Museum (Additional Manuscripts, 19,377) will be surprised at either Mr. White's or Mr. Murray's acceptance of them. The correspondence consists of letters to Douglas Kinnaird, Sir G. Webster and Sir James Mackintosh, Colonel Hay, Shelley and others between 1812 and 1824. The letters have the foreign postmarks of Venice, Ravenna, or Pisa, as the case may be; the seals, the addresses, the handwriting, the signature, all seem to be above suspicion.

But it is the tone and style of these letters no less than the actual handwriting which are so marvellously Byronic. The characteristic wit and bitterness of the poet are absent from none of the letters, and such internal evidence was decidedly in favour of their genuineness. Take, for example, this to Sir J. Mackintosh :—

"Rhyming is as easy as punning to one who will allow his thoughts to run more by the associations of sound than of sense. . . . Sometime in the course of his life, under the influence of love, madness, or some other calamity, almost every one is silly enough to sin in rhyme."

Or to Kinnaird about an incident in Galignani :—

" Because an accident happened to occur the other day by a horse taking fright at the squeaking of Mr. Punch, some of these strait-waistcoat-mongers are for having our merry old friend put down by Act of Parliament."

It is only, however, by a perusal of the whole collection that a real idea can be formed of their extraordinarily life-like character—a character which could only have been impressed upon them by great ability combined with an intimate knowledge of the poet's actual life. Both these qualifications belonged in an eminent degree to the supposed writer of the letters, Icodad George Gordon Byron, who claimed to be the natural son of the poet by a Spanish lady and who supported his claim by a very remarkable facial resemblance.

There seems no reason to doubt that this Byron had taken great pains to collect materials for a new Life of his alleged father ; he had travelled abroad with this object, and had solicited letters of Lord Byron from all probable quarters. Early in 1848 he had notified in the press this forthcoming Life, containing unpublished letters of the poet, to which he had had access through the kindness of Mrs. Leigh, the poet's sister. But unfortunately on 1st April, 1848, this said Mrs. Leigh wrote a letter to the *Athenæum*, denying such access on the part of Byron, and throwing doubt on his claim to be the son of the poet. A letter from a firm of solicitors of 24th March, 1848, also drew attention to the falsity of some of Byron's pretensions, and consequently the projected Life was never published in England. It would appear that it was shortly after this exposure that the lady paid her first visit to Mr. White, with a view to turning the letters to profitable account.

But even after the forty-seven letters had been sold to Mr. White, Byron persevered with his intention of bringing out a Life of his father. In August, 1849, he returned to America, and there again notified to the world a most attractive work : *The Inedited Works of Lord Byron, now first published from his letters, journals, and other manuscripts, in the possession of his son Major George Gordon Byron.* The work was to come out in twenty monthly parts, beginning 1st October, 18.49. In this announcement, signed by George Gordon Byron, Publisher, 237 Broadway, New York, Byron claimed to possess about 1,000 letters of the poet, and his *Ravenna Journal* of 1822. The two first numbers duly appeared, but most of his materials had been left in England, and his inability to obtain them caused the work to be discontinued, and threw Byron into a state of despair.

It was indeed no common work that Byron had projected, nor any common industry that he had bestowed upon its completion. " Every book he could meet with," says Mr. Sotheby, " containing matter

that could be turned to account by him, was carefully
read by him ; all the various periodicals of the time
were ransacked ; no source of information he could
in any way obtain was neglected." Had the book
only been successfully launched, it would have gone
far to bring its author both fame and fortune.

But Byron had a wife, who it seems reasonable
to suppose accompanied him to America in August,
1849. And it must have been some time in 1848
that Mr. White had made the discovery that his
mysterious lady, who had sold him the letters, was
none other than Mrs. Byron. There was no invalid
sister nor a surgeon in the case at all. Mr. White
tells us how, his suspicions being aroused, he
challenged the lady's story, and how she confessed ;
and how the next day Byron himself came with his
wife ; showed him in print part of his father's Life ;
said he had bought many of his Byron letters from
Mr. Hodges of Frankfurt and of Mr. Wright of the
Quarterly Review ; had acquired the books from
Fletcher ; and the Shelley letters in various ways,
some of them from the box left behind at Marlow
when Shelley moved from that place. He also
signed a written attestation of their genuineness.

This appears to have satisfied Mr. White, in
spite of the false story of which he had been the
victim. Otherwise it is impossible to account for
his having sold to Mr. Murray some months after
his discovery of Byron, and without any allusion to
him, letters acquired under conditions so suspicious.

It is no less surprising to find him a year later, in August, 1850, sending to Messrs. Sotheby to be sold by auction the Shelley letters which he had obtained from the same tainted source that had supplied him with the Byron letters. Besides these were books enriched with Byron's signature and notes, and also seven letters and a poem by Keats. The sale took place in the May of 1851, and resulted in some very high prices ; Mr. Moxon, the publisher, being the happy purchaser of the Shelley letters for £115 4s. 6d.

At the same sale were some scandalous letters from Shelley to his wife, containing unfilial statements about the poet's father. These were probably the letters which Mr. White, acting under Mr. Moxon's advice, had previously tried to dispose of to Mrs. Shelley, incurring her wrath for what she thought was an attempt to extort money, and these were bought in by Sir Percy Shelley and never became public.

But with those bought by Mr. Moxon it was otherwise. In 1852 Mr. Moxon ushered into the world a most interesting little book of *Letters of Percy Bysshe Shelley, with an Introductory Essay by Robert Browning*. The letters were twenty-five in number, covering the years between 1811 and 1821, and Browning's marvellous Introduction constituted a fourth part of the volume. It is full of incoherent language and of strange metaphors, as where we read of a poet " who shall at once replace this in-

tellectual rumination of food swallowed long ago by
a supply of the fresh and living swathe," but all that
Browning claimed to do was to facilitate the writing
of Shelley's biography "by arranging these few
supplementary letters, with a recognition of the value
of the whole collection". This value he took to con-
sist in the "most truthful conformity of the Correspondence, in its limited degree, with the moral and
intellectual character of the writer as displayed in
the highest manifestations of his genius".

But alas! for human fallibility; for this "most
truthful conformity," proving that Shelley's poetical
mood was "only the intensification of his habitual
mood," had nothing to do with Shelley at all. It
was probably all due to the clever hand and brain of
George Gordon Byron. Twenty-three out of these
twenty-five letters are bound up in the same volume
with the Byron letters in the British Museum.
Though written by the same hand they are in a
totally different handwriting from the Byron letters,
being of course as true to that of Shelley as they are
to his tone and habit of thought. They seemed to
stand every test; they were written from places
where Shelley was known to have been at the dates
prefixed to them. Mr. Moxon had accepted them
as genuine; what reason had Browning to doubt
them?

Indeed it was due to pure chance that any one
ever came to doubt them. Moxon *happened* to send
a copy of the published letters to Tennyson; Pal-

grave *happened* to be staying with Tennyson ; and
in turning over the leaves, Palgrave *happened* to re-
cognise a passage which he remembered as occurring
in a *Quarterly Review* article by his father, Sir
Francis Palgrave, so long ago as the year 1840.
The details appeared in the *Literary Gazette* of
28th February, 1852, and were sent to that periodical
after a most favourable notice of the letters in the
preceding number (21st Feb.) wherein the letters had
been described as " charming and valuable ".   It is
somewhat startling to think that but for the coincidence of all these unlikely contingencies the forged
Shelley letters might have furnished material for a
falsified biography of him to the end of time.

No sooner had Mr. Moxon become aware of the
fraud than he suppressed the publication, and called
in the copies he had issued to the trade.   Detection in
this case had come speedily.   It was on 21st February,
1852, that the *Athenæum* had published a review of
the book, and on 6th March it cried out " Forgery ".
All the letters, with one or two unspecified excep-
tions, it pronounced to be fabrications.   The post-
marks on the letters had been compared with those
on Byron's genuine letters, sent to Mr. Murray from
the same places and at the same dates, and it had
been discovered that the postmarks from Venice and
Ravenna on the Shelley letters differed intrinsi-
cally from those on the genuine letters.

More important and conclusive was the discovery
that the following characteristic passage in a letter

from Shelley to Graham had been taken, with hardly
the change of a word, from an article entitled
" Thoughts on Bores " by a Bore, in *Janus*, an Edinburgh Literary Almanac of the year 1826 (p. 73) :—

"But the cerulean blue—the true celestial—she
who really has heaven in her eye, follow her to the
world's end. Love her! Adore her! You must and
will. Win her and wear her if you can. She is the
most delightful of God's creatures—Heaven's best
gift ; man's joy and pride in prosperity ; man's support and comforter in affliction. I know there are
unbelievers who would class my true celestials among
fabulous creatures. I own they are rare."

It is, however, to be noted in the interests of those
who may possess or who may acquire this instructive
little volume that the twenty-third letter in the series
to Keats, advising and inviting him to spend the
winter in Italy, is a genuine Shelley letter. At least
a Westminster reviewer declared himself to have
been the possessor of such a letter for many years, a
copy of it having been printed by him in an article
on Keats in the *British Quarterly* for November, 1848
(*Westminster Review*, April, 1852, 503).

The suggestion that Byron simply copied this
letter is hardly consistent with the fact that, if he had
not already sold his Shelley letters to Mr. White
before November, 1848, it was about that time that he
sold them. A forger would be needlessly bold who
would take from a magazine of the current quarter
such a letter as this one to Keats to palm off on a pur-

chaser.   By what means this letter to Keats found
its way into the collection remains a mystery.

The letter also, No. 10, to Thomas Hookham,
dated 3rd August, 1816, is, like the letter to Keats,
absent from the collection presented to the British
Museum by Mr. White.

This double exposure of plagiarism was of course
fatal to the credit of the Shelley letters, and almost fatal
to that of Mr. White, against whom the *Athenæum*
had made some caustic remarks, almost insinuating
that he had been a party to the fraud.   To this charge
Mr. White replied in a printed letter to Mr. Murray,
dated 11th March, 1852, and published under the title
of *Calumnies of the "Athenæum Journal" Exposed.*
He explained his share in the transaction, and how
completely he had been deceived by "the speciousness
and the simplicity" of the lady who had brought him
these literary pearls.   But he omitted to mention the
date at which good reasons had occurred for his
suspecting the genuineness of the Byron letters he
had sold to Mr. Murray.   His main contention was
that letters which had deceived such authorities as
Mr. Murray and Mr. Moxon made excusable the
deception of himself.

To this the *Athenæum* replied, that the whole
trouble would have been avoided had Mr. White
once mentioned to either publisher the name of the
pseudo-Byron.   And, whilst acquitting Mr. White of
having been an accomplice of Byron, it pointed out
that Mr. White must have sold for some 300 guineas

what had not cost himself more than 100. It is due, however, to Mr. White's memory to add that he ultimately repaid to Mr. Murray and Mr. Moxon the sums they had paid for the forgeries.

Mr. Murray also replied to Mr. White in a letter dated 17th March, 1852, and printed in the *Literary Gazette* of 20th March. He denied that he had known anything of the connexion of Byron with the letters; had he done so, he would have hesitated to buy them. "I cannot account," he went on, "for your conduct in concealing from me all mention of his name until the week before last when I called on you to tell you that I had ascertained that they were forgeries."

From which are deducible two strange facts in this strange story : (1) that Mr. White sold the letters to Mr. Murray without mentioning that the lady, whose manner had been "so artless, open and candid," as to disarm all his anxiety, had been ascertained by himself to be the wife of a notoriously suspicious literary character ; (2) that Mr. Murray, having bought the letters in April, 1849, did not discover till March, 1852, that they were forgeries.

It remains extremely difficult to reconcile Mr. White's asseverations of his innocence in the matter with the facts as given in his own defence—a defence which is marked by a remarkable avoidance of all dates. Knowing the trickery that had been practised on himself, and with misgivings clearly aroused by such knowledge, he ought never to have sold the

Byron letters to Murray in 1849, nor in 1850 have
sent the letters of Shelley and Keats and the remainder of his purchases to be sold by auction.

The life as well as the origin of Byron remain
shrouded in considerable mystery. It would seem
that his claim to be an illegitimate son of Lord Byron
was first made in a letter to Mr. Murray, dated 1st
July, 1843, written from Pennsylvania. Only embar-
rassing circumstances compelled him to disclose to a
friend of the late Lord Byron the secret of his birth.
His mother had belonged to an old noble Spanish
family, and, though a Catholic herself, had consigned
her son to a Protestant tutor to be educated as a Protestant. Then came years at college which "glided
away in unperturbed tranquillity". From Paris he returned to Spain with "an indescribable passion for adventure from childhood which it required even the
stimulus of danger to satisfy". Then his mother died,
leaving him only her diamonds; after which he started
on a pilgrimage to all the places "rendered sacred
by the temporary residence of Lord Byron". From
Greece he roved over the East ; "from the city of the
Sultan to the Pyramids and Cataracts of the Nile ;
from Mount Ararat to the mouth of the Ganges".
Returning thence to Spain, Byron took some part in
the political struggles of that country, but after disap-
pointment in this direction he went to America, where
he bought a farm near Wilkes Barre in the classic
valley of Wyoming. For a time everything promised
fair, till a sudden commercial crisis deprived him of

the little fortune he had left, and compelled him to appeal to the friends of Lord Byron for a loan to pay the next instalment of the purchase-money of his farm.

Such a letter with such a claim belongs to a not unfamiliar type, and the amount of truth in it cannot be gauged. But the marvellous resemblance of his features and to some extent of his handwriting with those of Lord Byron undoubtedly lent countenance to his story, and Mr. Sotheby, who was sceptical at first, inclined ultimately to the opinion that Byron was really the son of the poet.

Actual proof that Byron was himself the forger of the Byron and Shelley letters is wanting. The similarity of his handwriting to that of Lord Byron, as shown in the facsimiles given in Mr. Sotheby's *Principia Typographica*, is perhaps not more than superficial. Mr. Sotheby was convinced in 1855 that all the forgeries were in one handwriting, but the Byron letters and the Shelley letters, to which must be added seven from Keats, were of course in the writing of their supposed authors, and therefore as different from one another as possible. Only the verdict of an expert in handwriting would avail to prove that all these letters were really in one handwriting, and such a verdict has never been given.

The trick and the falsehood employed by Byron in disposing of these letters to Mr. White raises of course the strongest suspicion against him, but for many years before that Byron had troubled all sorts of people for letters of Lord Byron : a proceeding hardly compatible with either the ability or the intention to produce such letters by forgery. Byron always claimed to have acquired by such solicitation or purchase about a thousand of Byron's letters, and, if this were true, he can have been under no absolute necessity to forge any, though pecuniary temptation may have led him to do so. It is known that Byron lived for some time in the same house with Mr. Wright, who had acted as sub-editor for Mr. Murray's edition of Lord Byron, and he may easily have received from Mr. Wright some Byronic letters which had been rejected as spurious. Although therefore the case is highly suspicious against Byron, it is not absolutely conclusive : the possibility cannot be precluded that in his search for autograph letters he was, like most collectors, himself the victim of the fraud of others.

In Sotheby's Sale Catalogue for May, 1851, may be found the titles of the works sold and the prices given for them by their several buyers in that memorable week's sale which began on 12th May. Interesting in the light of later knowledge are the auctioneers' comments on these highly prized letters of Shelley and Keats, especially on those eleven letters to Mrs. Shelley which were bought in by the Shelley family for £57 15s. The presumption is that, if the letters bought by Mr. Moxon were forgeries, these would fall under the same condemnation, whether forged by Byron or by some person unknown ; but the fact remains undecided.

The seven letters of Keats fell into different hands, being sold for £13 19s. Lord Houghton bought a few of them, and also a poem, which he subsequently published, as of doubtful authenticity, in an appendix to his *Life and Letters of Keats* (360). If not authentic, he wrote, it was a clever imitation, and Lord Houghton leant to the opinion that it was authentic, and contended that it was unjust to condemn as fraudulent all that had been sold on that famous occasion.

The whole story affords a standing warning against the pleasant folly of collecting autographs. Assuming these letters to have been forged, they are miraculous illustrations of what can be accomplished in that line. They prove that artificial literature can be produced as readily as artificial pearls, to the deceiving even of the ablest experts. No one living knew the handwriting of Byron and Shelley better than Mr. Murray and Mr. Moxon respectively, yet they were completely deceived by a resemblance which applied not merely to the actual handwriting but to the very minds of the two authors who were imitated.

The discovery of the fraud was due rather to hazard than to the sagacity of any one concerned. What hope can there be therefore for the ordinary collector or buyer of such wares?

CHAPTER XI.

A GERMAN FORGER: FRIEDRICH WAGENFELD.

A BREAST of triple brass must be his who ventures on an imposition with the learned world in Germany. Yet this boldness must be placed to the credit of Wagenfeld, who in his twenty-fifth year (1835) tried to palm off on his contemporaries a work which, had it only been genuine, would have constituted the greatest historical discovery of the nineteenth century.

Wagenfeld had been a student of theology and philosophy at Gottingen for four years (1829-1832), and in the course of his studies had doubtless become acquainted with the *Evangelica Præparatio* of Eusebius. In the first book of this work are somewhat copious extracts from Porphyry's lost work against the Christians, containing passages from an alleged Greek translation by Philo Byblius of the nine books of the history composed by the Phenician Sanchoniathon.

Sanchoniathon (whose name meant the Lover of Truth) had, in a time before the Trojan War, collected all the ancient history of Phenicia from monuments supplied by its several towns, and had related

with the greatest exactitude all that related to the
Jews from the memoirs of the priest Jerombal. This
history had been dedicated to Abibal, King of Berytus, and after examination by alleged competent judges
accepted as true. It was this history which Philo
Byblius had translated from Phenician into Greek.

Eusebius quotes extracts from Philo's preface to
the first book of his translation, telling how Sanchoniathon had studied the writings of Taautos, the
inventor of letters, and the secret writings of the
Ammonians ; and then gives several most interesting pages about the cosmogony and theology of the
Phenicians. But there is unfortunately nothing more
in Eusebius of Sanchoniathon's history.

Here therefore was a gap in the history of the
world that sorely needed closing up. What would
the world not give to know more about the early
history of that great and mysterious Phenician race ?
What would it not give to possess again in its en-
tirety the lost books of Philo's translation of Sanchoniathon (assuming that such a work had ever
existed). And in the thirties of the last century the
researches of the learned Gesenius at Gottingen had
renewed public interest in the history of Phenicia.

What finer opportunity could have been offered
to a man of vivid imagination and of irreproachable
Greek scholarship ? But imagine a young man of
twenty-five not quailing before the task of reproduc-
ing in Greek the lost books of Philo's translation
adapted to the model of the few pages in Greek

preserved of Philo in Eusebius. Yet it was no less a task than this to which young Wagenfeld addressed himself: surely one of the boldest literary labours ever undertaken. And, if anything could have justified the attempt, it was the ability displayed in it.

Wagenfeld appears to have begun his assault on German credulity by a letter to G. H. Pertz, the celebrated historian, dated 18th October, 1835, purporting to have come from Oporto, from a certain John Pereiro, knight. It was written in Latin, and told how in the monastery of Santa Maria de Merinhao, situated between the rivers Duero and Minho, the complete nine books of Philo's translation, of which Eusebius had only preserved the imperfect remains of one, had been found in a perfect state. The writer begged that the learned world should be acquainted with news of the discovery. On 30th October, 1835, the Hanover *Zeitung* announced it.

This was followed by a second Latin letter from Pereiro to Wagenfeld in November of the same year, purporting to send the MS., but asking him not to publish it at present, except in an epitome, and to show the Greek MS. to no one. The reason was, that the happy finder was at some difference with the monks, who, willing at first to let Pereiro have the MS. for a mere trifle, had raised their price to £50. But this letter was signed Pereir*a*, not Pereir*o*.

Wagenfeld's connexion with Pereiro was supposed to have been made through Pereiro's nephew,

13

who was said to have resided at Bremen during the summer of 1835 and to have helped Wagenfeld to learn Portuguese. What then more natural than for the nephew to inform Wagenfeld of his uncle's wonderful discovery, or for the uncle, on his nephew's advice, to send Wagenfeld the work? The MS. had been found not in the library of the cloister, but in a box in a cupboard of the room in which Pereiro chanced to be lodging. Three other MSS., afterwards corrected by the uncle to thirteen, had also been found in the same wonderful box.

These facts appeared in a letter to the publishing firm of the brothers Hahn at Hanover, dated 16th January, 1836. Wagenfeld's first letter to them, suggesting the publication of the more important parts of the discovered translation, was dated 20th December, 1835, and was signed Wilde. In a subsequent letter, when he had succeeded in persuading the learned Oriental scholar G. L. Grotefend to write a preface to his epitome of Sanchoniathon, he excused himself for having used his mother's name for a pseudonym ; he could not find it in his conscience to let "the worthy Director Grotefend" sign his name to a work issued pseudonymously. And in another letter of January, whilst expressing regret that the injunctions of Pereiro prevented him from sending Grotefend the Greek MS., he alluded to his readiness to send him two other MSS., if Grotefend was interested in mediæval literature. One of these was a copy of the *Sachsenspiegel* in Low German of the fourteenth century; the other was a hymn to the Virgin by "poor Conrad".

It appears from a letter to Grotefend himself of 27th February, 1836, that the first of these was actually sent to him by Wagenfeld. He sent it as a sign of his gratitude for the kind reception Grotefend had vouchsafed to his Phenician discovery. Was it one of the thirteen MSS. found in the same box with the Philo Byblius? In that case it looks as if Wagenfeld had contemplated a whole series of forgeries to follow the one already in hand; but his memory is so heavily burdened with the forgery he accomplished that those which never emerged from conception may be suffered to lie lightly upon him.

By the middle of April Grotefend was in possession of Wagenfeld's epitome, together with a short facsimile of the clearly preserved Greek original. The preface he wrote is dated 24th May, 1836, and its connexion with the "Early History of the Phenicians" (*Urgeschichte der Phœnizier*) affords a melancholy but amusing illustration of the occasional fallibility of the learned. For Grotefend, one of the most learned men of his time, was completely deceived. He expressed his delight at the discovery of this oldest known history of Phenicia. There was no name, no incident, in Wagenfeld's purely fictitious history which he did not accept with the most childlike faith. Some of the Phenician legends, he argued, must have been the source of certain passages in Genesis. A certain hymn over Sidon, in which that

13 *

city is compared to a pearl or to a star fallen from
heaven, was comparable, in his esteem, to the prophet
Ezekiel's song over the fall of Tyre.   Only the Phenician poetry struck him as being of higher order
than might have been expected of so commercial a
people : it had a marked tendency to the elegiac.
He appears in short to have accepted the forgery,
not only implicitly but with enthusiasm.

For him the story was true of King Joram having
an account of the Phenician expedition to Ceylon
(which was identified of course with Ophir) inscribed
on a pillar in the temple of Melicertes at Tyre; whereon
was also inscribed a most elaborate account of the
military strength of the various cities and colonies of
Phenicia, and some account of the countries they
traded with.   Joram had four copies of this inscrip-
tion taken and sent to other cities.   But when an
earthquake had destroyed the pillar, and the four
copies had also perished, Sanchoniathon resolved to
copy it verbatim from the fallen pillar.   This copy
was called " the Periplus of Joram," and Wagenfeld
had felt it to be so important that he gave it word
for word in German in the eighth book of Sanchoniathon.

This Phenician writer was now discovered to
have been the son of Kusabas, and the grandson of
Okalathon, both writers to the king ; and he wrote
his history about the middle of the ninth century B.C.
In this he frequently referred to his sources and
authorities, such as the Books of Taaut, the Deeds of

Bethebalus, the Songs of Nama, and so forth. And
he told some wonderful things : of Titans, half-naked
savages, who obtained white horses from Media, and
worshipped them as gods, and whom Grotefend readily
identified with certain people mentioned by Ezekiel ;
of giants who frequently fought with the Phenicians,
and on one occasion were destroyed by fire from
heaven ; of two marvellous horses, called Dolixurus
and Mira ; of a miraculous equestrian virgin ; of a
priest of Saturn who in the reign of Garusaus lived for
many years without touching food ; of another priest
of Egyptian origin who was the inventor of scythed
chariots for use in war ; of King Leonturgus who
used to go round the watch at night and kill any
sentinels he might find drunk ; of Damascon, an
exile from Egypt, who fought for King Bimalus and
afterwards founded the city of Damascus.

There were the names of all the kings of Sidon
and of Býblos for a long period. Grotefend drew up
a list of twenty-one kings of Sidon, and of fifteen in
Byblos, and attempted a comparative chronology of
their dates. He was also able from the " Periplus "
to draw up an accurate table of the total military and
naval resources of all the Phenician cities and of their
colonies ; of the latter there were ten in number, four
in Rhodes, two in Cyprus, two in Liguria, one in
Malta and one in Crete. All which would have
been vastly interesting and a valuable addition to the
knowledge of the world, if only it had been true.
One can imagine the inventor's glee at having his

astonishing history accepted as undoubtedly genuine by such an authority as G. F. Grotefend.

But Grotefend's son, Karl Ludwig, did not share his father's easy faith. He published in September, 1836, a short but pertinent pamphlet, called *The Sanchoniathon Question*, in which he printed all the letters which had been written in connexion with the supposed Phenician find : two Latin letters from the supposed Portuguese Pereiro ; seven letters from Wagenfeld, either in his own name or under the pseudonym of Wilde, to the publishers Hahn ; and one from Wagenfeld to Grotefend, his father. This collection of hitherto unpublished letters went far to ruin the forgery.

But the elder Grotefend was not the only one to believe at first in the false Sanchoniathon. Gesenius, his equal in learning, who had published learned works on Phenicia, told Wagenfeld in a letter that he considered it almost impossible that the work could be a forgery. He was much struck by the identity of many of the proper names in Wagenfeld's work with real Phenician names, such as he himself had found on inscriptions. This would have been remarkable in itself, had it not been explicable by the fact that Gesenius' own work on the Phenician and Punic writing, published in 1835, afforded an easy mine from which to draw real Phenician names.

But the other learned men in Germany were of a more sceptical turn of mind. Dr. Schmidt of Bremen

told how on one interview with Wagenfeld he was
informed that he could not see the Greek MS.,
because it had been sent back to Pereiro, and how
on another occasion he was informed that the MS.
was still in Wagenfeld's possession but would not be
shown to him.   Wagenfeld had also been unable to
give the name of Pereiro's nephew.   Schmidt also
wondered why Sanchoniathon, whom Porphyry had
assigned to Berytus, and Suidas to Tyre, should now
be assigned to Byblos; and why Buddhism, which
only began in the sixth century B.C., should have
been found in Ceylon in the eleventh.   And the first
Latin letter from Oporto bore the Bremen postmark,
and was written on paper clearly made at Osnabruck
in Germany.

The younger Grotefend also learnt from a friend
in Portugal that there was no such cloister as the
alleged one, and that the whole of Portugal did not
possess an officer of any sort who could write a letter
in Latin.   Pereiro, too, was unknown as a Portuguese
name ; it was always Pereira.

But the extraordinary fact remains that in spite
of all these discoveries, which discredited the work in
the esteem of all who were competent to judge,
Wagenfeld persevered, and in the spring of the
following year (1837) published his Greek version of
Philo Byblius' supposed translation, with a Latin
translation opposite to every page in Greek.   The
full title was : *Sanchoniathonis Historiarum Pheni-
ciæ Libros Novem Græce versos a Philo Byblio edidit*

Latineque versione donavit F. Wagenfeld. Bremæ 1837, *ex officina Caroli Schunemanni.*

This courageous work, containing some 205 pages, is for its great curiosity well worth possessing. K. O. Muller, as soon as it appeared, wrote a most damaging criticism of its claim to authenticity in the *Gottingische Gelehrte Anzeige* (1st April, 1837), but he admitted that the extreme cleverness of the work entitled its author to some admiration. It was no mean task to write nine books of Greek, adapted to the style of Philo Byblius as deducible from the extracts from his work given in Eusebius' *Præparatio Evangelica;* and, in spite of some mistakes, this task the author had accomplished with considerable success. He had also caught the spirit of the ancient historians, and by a judicious mixture of fable with his supposed facts given an air of verisimilitude to the whole which was well calculated to deceive even the elect in the learned world.

This criticism by Muller virtually settled the question. Gesenius, who shortly afterwards brought out his work on the *Monuments of the Phenician Writing and Language*, explained in his preface that he had never attached more than slender credit to Wagenfeld's discovery, and that subsequent criticism, since he had become possessed of the Greek version, had shattered his faith in it entirely. The work had no friend, nor did Grotefend, the elder, again act as its sponsor by writing a preface.

Muller concluded his article by the expression of

a good-natured wish that Wagenfeld might in the future employ the great abilities and learning, of which he had given such brilliant proofs, in the service of knowledge more useful to others and more honourable to himself; but this wish was never fulfilled. For some years Wagenfeld's life remained a literary blank, and the demon of drink is said to have taken possession of him. In 1845 he published, however, an interesting collection of the Legends of Bremen (*Bremen's Volksagen*), and in the year following a volume on the Military Expeditions of the people of Bremen (*Kriegsgefährten der Bremer*). That same year he died, at the early age of thirty-six. He is at least entitled to the fame, whatever his motive may have been, of having attempted one of the ablest and most daring fabrications in the history of literature, and of having made his victim for a time one of the most learned men in the learned world of Germany. Possibly he had no other motive; possibly he achieved his aim. And he certainly showed with what comparative ease the purest fiction may be dressed in the garb of truth, and romance be substituted for history.

CHAPTER XII.

A FRENCH FORGER: VRAIN-DENIS LUCAS.

THE prince of forgers, as regards quantity, hails from France. England may make some boast of her Chatterton or her Ireland, but it is to compare pigmies with giants to mention these youths in the same breath with Vrain-Denis Lucas, born in 1818 at Chateaudun in France, and the son of a peasant. A very common education was his, but he supplemented it by frequenting the library of his native place in the leisure he could win from his work in a lawyer's office. When he left Chateaudun for Paris in 1852, in his thirty-fourth year, he started with every prospect and promise of success.

But fortune frowned on him. Failing to obtain a post in the Imperial Library or with a publisher, he became associated with the establishment of M. Letellier, whose function it was to feed the vanity of certain classes with the provision of pedigrees and titles, not always of historical value. There appears to be the same demand for that sort of thing in France which exists in England. The Marquis de Du Prat would fain find something to connect him with Cardinal Du Prat of the sixteenth century for

a contemplated work on the family history; could
Lucas produce nothing? The temptation was obvious, and the career of the forger had begun. Lucas
soon produced two letters from Montaigne, one to
Antoine de Du Prat, Provost of Paris, another to
the Marquis de Nantouillet. Of these letters the
Marquis de Du Prat was kind enough to give facsimiles to M. Feuillet de Conches, one of the chief
collectors of autographs in France and one of the
greatest experts on the subject. In 1854 M. de
Conches published his *Causeries d'un Curieux* in
four volumes, wherein he unsuspiciously printed
these letters from Montaigne with judicious remarks
on the light they threw on the history of their time
(iii., 242). It failed to strike him that Montaigne
in one letter wrote *aristogratique* for *aristocratique*;
and a strange word *doloir* he thought must be peri-
gordian or gascon.

If this was Lucas' first essay, it must have been
vastly encouraging. With such success with one
expert, what might he not hope from others? We
may guess he was not idle between 1854 and 1861,
when he first began his operations on M. Chasles, a
man of world-wide reputation as a geometrician and
astronomer. On M. Chasles between 1861 and
February, 1870, when Lucas was sentenced by the
Correctional Tribunal of Paris to two years' imprisonment and a fine of £25, as many as 27,320 forged
letters were successfully palmed off, at a price to
their dupe of nearly £6,000—one of the most colossal

frauds ever perpetrated. The logical incapacity that
M. Chasles displayed throughout the contest subsequently waged over his supposed treasures shows
conclusively how insignificant is the benefit conferred
on the reasoning faculties by mathematical studies.
The leading mathematician of his country showed
himself incapable of reasoning better than a child.
Whenever any doubt was thrown on a particular
letter, he invariably met it by referring to some other
letter of equally doubtful authenticity.

From 1861 to 1869 M. Chasles continued to purchase letters of surpassing scientific and historical
interest from Lucas, and occasionally hundreds at a
time. But how had Lucas come by them? The
story was that a certain Comte de Boisjourdain before
the Revolution had been a great collector of autograph letters ; his collection included some five or
six thousand given to him by Louis XVI., when there
were other things to think about than autographs.
Becoming an *émigré* to America in 1791, he suffered
shipwreck and perished, but the greater part of his
invaluable collection, after some days' immersion in
the sea, had been recovered in a fair condition, and
at that time was in the hands of a descendant of
Boisjourdain, an old gentleman, who set a high value
on the letters, and would never part with one of them
before reading it. But he needed money, and therefore he had instructed Lucas to dispose of them at a
commission of 25 per cent. Behind this old gentleman was another, an old military relative, whose

consent to such sale had in some measure to be obtained and who showed himself rather averse from parting with them ; in fact so averse was he, that on one occasion the heir of all the Boisjourdains expressed through Lucas a wish to have the letters back, offering for their return all the money M. Chasles had paid for them. This offer removed from M. Chasles' mind every shadow of a doubt of the veracity of Lucas, and of course whetted his appetite for more of his treasures.

There are perhaps few of us who can fairly throw a stone at M. Chasles for his credulous acceptance of this amazing story.

In 1867 it became known that M. Chasles purposed to publish a book on the Discovery of the Laws of Attraction by Pascal, and on 8th July he promised to lay before the Academy of Sciences, of which he had been a prominent member since 1851, the letters on which he based a claim so flattering to the pride of his countrymen, and so damaging to that of a neighbouring island which had always claimed the discovery of the Laws of Gravitation for her Sir Isaac Newton. A week later he read to his colleagues two letters from Pascal to Robert Boyle which in his opinion proved his case ; for it was not till 1687 that Newton had made his discovery, and these letters bore the earlier date of 1652.

Great of course was the excitement, nor was it to abate for two years, during which it was destined to distract and divide the world of learning both in

France and abroad.   Fresh letters came pouring in
week by week and month by month, till, in all, the
Comptes Rendus of the Academy possessed as many
as 381.   Nothing would induce M. Chasles to say
from what source he had derived them, and he re-
solutely refused to compare the signature of Pascal
in the new letters with the undoubted signature of
Pascal at the Imperial Library.   He sent photo-
graphic copies of some Pascal-Newton letters to Sir
David Brewster, who had written much on Newton,
and who at once pronounced the letters spurious.
There was one from Pascal to Newton when a
scholar at Grantham, aged eleven, in which Pascal
exhorted his young friend to work and study, but
with moderation ; it was only knowledge so acquired
which was profitable.   But no proof that it was not
till a much later age that Newton studied scientific
questions at all had any effect upon M. Chasles.

And there were sceptics as wicked as Brewster
in France itself.   From the first M. Faugère, celebrated for his works on Pascal, proclaimed the letters
to be forgeries, and the same honour belongs to M.
Bénard de Champs of Evreux.   This, in M. Chasles'
view, showed a lamentable want of patriotism, and a
disgraceful leaning to the English enemy.   There was
no *entente cordiale* in those days, and the patriotic
argument influenced even M. Thiers on the side of
the forgeries.

But, despite the sceptics, faith in the genuineness
of the letters increased, as they poured in from all

sorts of persons of distinction. The Academy of Sciences itself, after a year and a half of trouble and disputations, gave a kind of official sanction to the letters on 5th April, 1869. There were letters of Louis XIV., whose noble simplicity no forger could have produced; the style of the letters proved that they could only have emanated from their professed authors; whilst their freedom from such blunders as no forger could have avoided were a moral proof of their authenticity. Such arguments have a familiar ring about them.

M. Chasles and Lucas must have been happy men when that report came to their knowledge. But the tide of human happiness is often on the turn when at its highest, and a week later came forward M. Breton to show that six precious notes by Pascal and two fragments of a letter by Galileo had been taken straight from Saverien's *Histoires des Philosophes Modernes* (1760-1773).

This was disconcerting, but M. Chasles at once replied that Saverien had borrowed from the letters, not the letters from Saverien. This was proved immediately by letters from Saverien to the Marquise de Pompadour, returning 200 letters from men of science like Pascal and Newton and Galileo, and alluding to the great service they had been to him in the production of his contemplated work on modern philosophers.

The versatility displayed by Lucas in thus meeting all critical objections by freshly forged letters was truly marvellous. A famous instance of this occurred in respect of a letter of Galileo to Pascal, dated 2nd January, 1641, wherein Galileo wrote : " I cannot write more, for my eyes are very tired. I am losing my sight. Do not forget to send me a description of your arithmetical machine." And in all the letters attributed to Galileo in that year was the same allusion to his failing sight. But there was abundant evidence that Galileo had been totally blind by the end of 1637. His own genuine letters proved it. Here again was a difficulty. But forthwith other letters were produced from Galileo, to show either that his blindness was of an intermittent kind, or that he had exaggerated it in order to pacify the Inquisition. This question of the blindness of Galileo provoked great discussion in the world of letters, but nothing shook M. Chasles' faith in the genuineness of the 3,000 letters of Galileo which he possessed, though the letters were written in French and Galileo never wrote but in Latin or Italian.

But light was at last to dawn even on Lucas' victim. On 21st June, 1869, M. Verrier began to read a Memoir which occupied four sittings of the Academy, and in which he showed the actual sources from which Lucas had borrowed the very terms of many of his letters. Saverien was not the only fountain : Voltaire had contributed, and Chauffepié's *Dictionary* (1750), and Père Gerdil, and Le Duc de la Vallière, and Thomas. For instance, in Thomas' *Éloge de Descartes* is the remark that the philosopher would have willingly remained unknown if only he could be useful, and this remark passed verbally into an alleged letter of Descartes to Queen Christina of Sweden of 2nd October, 1650. In fact whole passages so passed into the same letter with scarcely any alteration.

Discoveries of this sort produced an effect. So did certain signatures of Galileo sent to Florence to be compared with the real signature. They were returned as spurious. Then on 13th September, 1869, even M. Chasles was obliged to bow to the force of the evidence. But he had some reason for refusing to believe that one man alone could have produced such an enormous mass of forged documents. Yet the experts who examined them found them all to be undoubtedly in the handwriting of one man.

Four days after M. Chasles had laid the whole story before his comrades Lucas was arrested; a few months later he was sentenced to imprisonment, and therewith he vanished from the knowledge of mankind. If he survived his term of two years, he left prison at the age of fifty-four. Perchance he lived to a ripe old age, and continued to flood the world with new forgeries.

There is something almost grotesque in the fact of a mere forger, a man of no real education, ignorant alike of Latin and mathematics, not only holding his own for two years against one of the most learned societies in the world, but coming within an ace of

14

conquering it. A little more and the history of the
world lay at the mercy of his unbridled fancy. On
so frail a tenure rests the kingdom of truth. And it
has to be admitted that there was something grandi-
ose in Lucas' endeavour. It is hardly possible to do
justice to the industry, the knowledge, the versatility,
the ability, displayed by him. They were almost
superhuman, and it is small wonder that M. Chasles
disbelieved the possibility of forgery on so gigantic
a scale. Lucas would have had to produce four
forged letters on each day of the seventeen years
he had spent in Paris to have completed the number
which he is known to have produced, but as it is
likely his most prolific period was in the eight years
when he had found a market for his wares, it is
probable that the rate of production was considerably higher than four a day. It is the enormous
output of his forgeries which differentiates him from
other workers in the same line.

The mere inventory of the false letters fills
seventeen closely printed pages in MM. Bordier
and Mabille's *Fabriques des Faux Autographes*
(51-68). There were over a thousand letters from
Pascal, including 175 to Sir Isaac Newton, 76 to
Boyle, 33 to Hobbes, and 139 to Galileo. There
were 27 letters from Shakespeare to Larivey; many
hundreds from Rabelais to various persons; in short
there was no name of distinction in the world's
history on which some letter or letters did not throw
fresh light and lustre. Nor were the letters con-

fined to modern times. There were letters of the
Roman emperors, letters from some of the Apostles,
ten letters from Plato, twenty-eight from Pliny, ten
from Seneca, one from Pompey to Cato. Nay, the
letters went farther back still. Thales and Anaxi-
menes and Anaximander contributed some portion of
their correspondence, nor does it appear to have
disconcerted M. Chasles that these most ancient
worthies wrote on paper and in the French language!
There were letters, too, from Lazarus to St. Peter;
from Mary Magdalene to Lazarus. This was her
letter to the King of the Burgundians :—

" Hail from Mary, sister of Martha and Lazarus :
accept my respects, together with this casket. In
it you will find the letter I spoke of to you which
was sent me by Jesus Christ a few days before His
passion. It is accompanied by two sentences which
constitute the basis of the religion of Christ. Take
good care therefore of these precious objects : so
you will be happy and live in peace, which is the
wish," etc.

Cleopatra thus writes to Cæsar :—

" Our son Cesarion is well. I hope he will soon
be able to bear the voyage to Marseilles, where I
design to have him educated as much for the good
air of the place as for the fine things they teach. I
beg you therefore to tell me how much longer you
will stay in those countries," etc.

Possibly M. Chasles did not read all his specimens, but accepted them in blind trust. Their

14 *

absurdities and their blunders, alike, seem to have escaped his notice. There were letters, for instance, from Strabo to Juvenal, though Strabo was ninety-two when Juvenal was born. There were letters from Bede to Alcuin, though Alcuin was only nine when Bede died. But considering that some thousand persons figured on Lucas' canvas, mistakes of this sort were marvellously few. In the 381 letters submitted to the Academy and filling 400 pages of its *Comptes Rendus* the only striking mistake occurred in a letter signed by the mother of Newton in her maiden name. But it was only the flower of the collection that was exhibited to the Academy, M. Chasles steadily refusing to show them the whole collection. Out of 3,000 letters of Galileo they only had 20 to deal with; out of 1,745 of Pascal only 80; out of 622 of Newton only 29. Had the whole been submitted to them, the French world of learning would have been spared some two years of acrimonious wrangling, and an exceedingly humiliating episode in its history.

Lucas posed as a patriot, and as a patriot he must be judged. In enriching himself he was studious to enhance the glory of France. The honour of France was to be subserved, not only by wresting from Newton to Pascal the fame of the discovery of the law of gravitation, but by recovering from the past all documents which redounded to the credit of Gaul. It was to its king, Ambigat, that Thales wrote his advice about government; Alexander the Great praised Gaul and its inhabitants in a letter to Aristotle; Lazarus wrote to St. Peter about the Druids of Gaul; Mary Magdalene wrote to the King of the Burgundians; Castor, a Gallic doctor, wrote a letter to Jesus Christ. One can imagine how all this might have enriched subsequent histories of France, had Lucas' false coin passed into historical currency.

Those must have been delightful years for M. Chasles in which he amassed these treasures of the past. The £6,000 he paid for them were a mere bagatelle for specimens so priceless. Nor was it only letters which he acquired, for Lucas also supplied him with books of incalculable value : genuine books, with the signature or a note of some famous owner forged at the beginning. M. Chasles became the possessor of 500 books that had once belonged to La Fontaine, Rabelais, and others. It may be questioned whether after all M. Chasles did not derive more pleasure from the acquisition of his collection than he suffered pain from the ultimate discovery of its worthlessness.

Lucas appears to have met his exposure with much real or simulated indifference. Almost to the eve of his arrest he frequented the public libraries in the pursuit of his art; and he fought the learned world gamely to the last. Nor was his line of defence destitute of humour. He declared his conscience to be calm; he had injured no one; he had recalled public attention to facts of history which had been in danger of being forgotten. Moreover, he had instructed and amused the public for two years during which it had found pleasure in frequenting the sittings of the Academy ; M. Chasles, too, had won a hearing which otherwise would never have been vouchsafed to him.   As for himself, he would always enjoy the consciousness of having acted, if not with wisdom, yet at least with uprightness and patriotism.

So true is Dr. Johnson's dictum that patriotism is often the last refuge of a scoundrel.

CHAPTER XIII.

THE MARIE-ANTOINETTE FORGERIES.

THE comparative success of Lucas' forgeries raises some uncomfortable reflections about autographs in general. The taste in France for collecting them began about 1814, and it has been calculated that between 1822 and 1835 some 12,000 were sold at public sales. But from 1836 to 1840 the commerce in autographs so far increased that as many as 11,000 were sold; between 1841 and 1845 as many as 15,000; between 1846 and 1859 as many as 32,000. And this was before Lucas had appeared on the scene.

Whence came this enormous supply? Direct theft from public libraries undoubtedly would account for many, but the greater part were the offspring of forgery. The demand gave rise to the supply. And as many of these letters would pass from owner to owner, and throw new and false light on historical characters, it is not pleasing to think to what a serious extent history may have come to be falsified by such means. Had Lucas' inventions succeeded in obtaining currency, they would have revolutionised history from Thales to his own time ; but what of the inventions by others that did pass current, and were not detected?

It would be impossible to follow all these forged letters into the chinks they have served to fill in history. There are probably few historical personages whose characters and actions have not been falsely coloured by information drawn from these poisoned wells. But as there is no character which forgery more completely made its prey than the unfortunate Queen Marie-Antoinette, it may suffice from her case alone to draw some conclusions as to the romances which have arisen in the same way round the names and memories of others who at the same time or earlier played their destined parts on the stage of the world.

Forgery began to gather round Marie-Antoinette even in her lifetime; primarily of course in the famous scandal of the Diamond Necklace. This episode had so close a connexion with the Revolution that it may almost be doubted whether, but for the schemings and forgeries of the notorious Madame la Comtesse de la Motte in the necklace affair, the Revolution itself might not have been averted or delayed. In the annals of intrigue is nothing bolder than this forgery of a Queen's signature to an order on a firm of jewellers to the amount of £64,000, and the concoction of a fictitious amatory correspondence between the Queen and Prince Louis Cardinal de Rohan. This correspondence was actually written by La Motte's accomplice, Reteaux de Villette, and was burnt after the famous trial in May, 1786. But it would seem that the Cardinal really believed that the Queen wrote him these letters, and that his own letters reached the Queen; and it is probable that La Motte won from him vast sums for her imagined services as an intermediary. That the Cardinal himself was rather dupe than accomplice in the fraud follows less from his own character or his acquittal by the Parlement than from the seeming absence of the pecuniary motive which suffices to account for the trickery of the others.

After the trial, resulting in La Motte being whipped, branded and imprisoned, and in Villette being banished, La Motte joined her husband in England, and there in 1788 she published her *Mémoires justificatifs*, containing thirty-one letters purporting to have passed between the Queen and the Cardinal. These she professed to have copied from the original correspondence which had been burnt. They revealed the Queen as directing the Cardinal how to disguise himself, and where to meet her; and were couched in terms highly discreditable to both parties. The Queen's genuine letters show the constancy and the intensity of her dislike of the Cardinal, and the pain which the whole affair caused her; but her memory had to wait a full century for its complete clearing, when in 1895 Maxime de la Rocheterie and the Marquis de Briancourt published their excellent collection of her genuine letters (*Receuil des Lettres Authentiques*). But in the meantime the Queen is reported to have been seen herself reading a manuscript copy of these terrible *Memoirs*, which ran through several editions and were last republished in 1846. Forgery in this case touched its lowest depths.

But many others besides La Motte and Villette had a hand in composing fictitious letters from the Queen. In such pamphlets as *The Queen Unmasked* (*La Reine Dévoilée*) in 1789, containing some alleged letters from her, and in the *Correspondence of the Queen with Illustrious Personages* (1790) political animosity was doubtless the inspiring motive. With letters of this sort she was confronted at her trial. When a witness declared that in September, 1792, he had found a letter from the Queen with the words "Can you count on your Swiss? Will they show up well when the time comes?" the Queen replied, "I have never written such a letter". And so with a letter she was said to have written to Bouillé to congratulate him on having had seven or eight thousand persons massacred at Nancy, the reply was, "I have never written to him". And then there was the false *Véritable lettre* addressed to the Convention, to the Departments of France and to foreign Powers, in which she denied the accusation of conspiring against the French people; charged them with having changed from a docile to a sanguinary people; reminded them of her charity to the poor; and expressed her desire for a reconciliation. There can be little doubt that forgery was a weapon which had a large share in her tragic fate.

But the intriguing La Motte perished before her victim. On the bailiffs entering her residence in London, she jumped out of window, but sustained such injuries that it took her several months to recover from them. When she had recovered, she died of a surfeit of mulberries (1791). Over the fate of Villette history maintains the silence of indifference.

But the production of forged letters was far from ceasing with the Queen's life. Three false letters of the Queen to the Princesse de Lamballe were printed (1801) in Madame Guénard's *Mémoires Historiques*, relating to that lady (iii., 222; iv., 138; iv., 167), and two in Lafond d'Aussonne's *Mémoires secrets . . . de la Reine de France* (89, 151), in 1824.

So the game of fabrication continued, the forging of letters keeping pace with the zeal of collectors. One is astonished to find Lucas not selling to M. Chasles more than seventeen letters of Marie-Antoinette; but there were other workers in the field besides Lucas, and other dupes besides M. Chasles. A proud man was the Count Paul Vogt d'Hunolstein when in 1864 he brought out, as the result of long autograph-hunting, such a work as the *Correspondance inédite de Marie-Antoinette, publiée sur les documents originaux*. There were 132 letters in all, covering a period of twenty-three years, from the year of the Queen's marriage in 1770 to the year preceding her death, 1792. The collector proceeded to give a sketch of the Queen's life and character, founded on this "instructive and touching correspondence," in which figured letters from the Queen to her mother Maria Theresa, to her brother Joseph II., to her sister Maria-Christina, and to several others. He was sure that writers more capable than himself would use these documents, which he had won for history, as precious materials for a new study of the Revolution.

History had rather a narrow escape from so unfortunate a fate. For the Count's book at once became popular, and was quickly followed by a second and third edition, incorporating nineteen fresh autograph letters of the Queen. But it so chanced that M. Feuillet de Conches, who had also been collecting autographs for twenty years and had consulted the archives of France, Austria, Russia and Sweden, brought out in the same year his work on the unpublished letters and documents of Louis XVI., Marie-Antoinette, and Mme. Elizabeth, and therein were twenty-four of the same letters that the Count had published, with certain slight differences in the text! Criticism was naturally roused ; the usual controversy ensued ; and attack and defence continued for more than two years.

In the course of this controversy M. d'Arneth published at Vienna from the private archives of the Imperial family the letters that had undoubtedly passed between the Queen and her mother between

1770 and 1780, and this supplied a standard of measurement for the questionable letters published by the two collectors of autographs. Facsimiles of the Queen's real signature showed marked differences from the doubtful signature. The forger, knowing only the Queen's signature of her later years, had provided all his works with a uniform signature, unaware of the modifications which the Queen's handwriting had assumed with time. Moreover there were historical and other contradictions with the Viennese letters. In short only two letters came unscathed out of the fire of criticism : one from the Queen to her mother dated 14th June, 1777, and one to Maria-Christina, dated 29th May, 1790, and both these were in the collection of M. Feuillet de Conches.

Nevertheless, in spite of criticism, the Count d'Hunolstein, in a long preface to the fourth edition of his collection, published in 1868, persevered in believing in the authenticity of his letters. To such a belief he had every reason to cling as long as possible. He had acquired all of his autographs, as M. Feuillet de Conches had acquired most of his, at public sales or by private purchase. M. Jacques Charavay, an expert and dealer in autographs, whose good faith in the matter was never doubted, had had dealings with both collectors ; and the Count had abundant reason for thinking it strange that M. Charavay should never have shown to M. Feuillet de Conches, through all their years of dealing, any of the letters he had sold to

himself! And the Count's collection was believed to
have stood him in a sum of £3,400! And who can
guess the sums paid by M. Feuillet de Conches, one
of the greatest collectors and experts in the world?

Some tribute is due to the skill of the unknown
forger of these letters. If they did not constitute
history, they followed historical lines, and were
founded on such historical works as the *Mémoires de
J. L. Soulavie* and of Mme. de Campan. They bore
a considerable likeness to the real letters of the Queen,
full of amiable sentiment and of concern for the health
of others and of herself. But the genuine letters convicted the writer of occasional mistakes, as where the
Queen is made to tell her sister that the " King, always
a slave to forms," had wished to submit to the Parlement the punishment of the Cardinal, after the
necklace affair, whereas the Queen's genuine letter
to Joseph II., dated 19th September, 1785, says expressly that "the King had the kindness to give the
Cardinal his choice between being judged by the
Parlement, or of admitting his crime and of submit-
ting himself to his clemency. He preferred the
former course, and it is said regrets it" (*cf.*
D'Hunolstein, 141, and Rocheterie's *Lettres*, ii., 78).

But if Count d'Hunolstein's collection failed to
give a false colour to history, the same cannot be
said of other letters of the Queen collected by other
collectors, and more especially by M. Feuillet de
Conches. In the course of the nineteenth century
twenty-nine letters of the Queen to the Duchesse de

Polignac came into circulation, most of which were published by De Conches, and eight of which belonged to him. These eight he seems to have obtained from a grocer, who had picked them up from the street when thrown out of a window of the royal stable, of which a Polignac was governor, by a victorious crowd in 1848! But some of De Conches' letters were in the collections of others, and it was found that whole passages had been extracted from genuine letters from the Queen to the Duchess, published by J. B. Gail in his *Lettres inédites* in 1828. Another source was the publication in 1796 by the Comtesse Diane de Polignac of the Memoirs of the Duchess, which contained extracts from the Queen's correspondence with her. These letters, belonging to the Polignac family, and copied by Gail, nine in all, are the only letters that can be accepted with any confidence as genuine, and all the history that has been built on the other twenty is so much waste-paper.

It is an extraordinary fact that so great an autographist as M. Feuillet de Conches should have failed to detect the numerous verbal identities between many of his letters and those which in 1828 had been published by Gail (Rocheterie's *Lettres*, Introd., xli.). He often lent some precious gems of his collection to friends who were occupied with historical works. He lent a Polignac letter to Beauchesne, in whose book on Louis XVII. it duly appeared in facsimile (i., 158), and he lent Lescure a number of letters from the Queen to the Princesse de Lamballe,

nor did the author of the life of that unfortunate
Princess use any other letters for his work but those
supplied him by De Conches. One of these, which
De Conches accounted among the most precious in
his collection, belonged to the three which by a late
legend fell out of her hair at the moment of her
assassination, and was stained with blood. But this
and forty other letters to the Princesse de Lamballe
are unauthentic, and render valueless all the histories
of which they form a part. To this category, in so
far as they are based on the Queen's letters, belong
both Lescure's *La Vraie Marie-Antoinette* and his
Princesse de Lamballe.

And in addition to these letters were a number
of others to different persons, which also came to
circulate amongst collectors and to pass from cabinet
to cabinet at public sales, at high prices. It would
be impossible to follow all these letters into the
crannies they may have come to occupy in history.
But the really genuine letters collected by Rocheterie
and the Marquis de Beaucourt amount to 396, and
these may be regarded as amply sufficing for the
needs of history.

When M. Geffroy was allowed to inspect the
Count's letters of the Queen to her mother and
sisters, it was at once apparent that there was not
the least similitude of writing between these letters
and the real ones; and it was admitted that M. de
Conches' letters were of a third variety of writing.
It was not a question of slight differences, difficult

to detect, and requiring the practised eye of an expert; it was a question "of a total difference" (*Gustave III. et la Cour de France*, ii., 328). But what an abyss this opens up! For here were men who made autographs their special hobby, who paid long prices for them, and who dealt with the most expert agents; yet purchasers and dealers were alike deceived by the superior skill of the professional forger. The only sane conclusion is to look with the gravest distrust on any letter purporting to be the Queen's in any private collection, especially if such letter is signed, for her more intimate letters were rarely signed; and in short to extend the same distrust to any letter purporting to be her husband's or that of any other historical character belonging to that time.

It may be thought that the triumph of the forger is apt to be transitory, and that truth will always emerge at last. But for this idea there is no foundation. Criticism with infinite trouble may succeed in exposing the falsity of certain letters, and of correcting the errors they have imported into history; but how can it deal with the enormous mass of such productions, or hope to drive from their historical position many a letter that has wrongfully crept into the confidence of mankind?

CHAPTER XIV.

THE IMMORTAL HOAX OF IRELAND.

NEVER in England has there been such a rush for places at a theatre as there was on Saturday, 2nd April, 1796, for places at Drury Lane. For it was the night when Sheridan was to present to the British public the famous play of " Vortigern and Rowena," the alleged recently discovered play of Shakespeare. Although Harris, of Covent Garden, had also offered liberal terms for the play, the competition had resulted in favour of Sheridan of Drury Lane, who agreed to pay the bookseller, Samuel Ireland, the possessor of the play, £300 down and half profits for the first sixty performances.

All the world has long since known that this wondrous play was in reality the sole composition of Ireland's son, William Henry, then a youth of barely eighteen years of age, who, at the time he first told his father of his find of a play of Shakespeare among the old papers belonging to the unknown gentleman " Mr. H.," had not only never attempted poetical composition of any sort, but had not even written a line of his marvellous composition.

Did Sheridan believe in its genuineness when he

put it on the stage? When he went to the book-seller's shop in Norfolk Street to inspect the fair copy, which had been transcribed from the MS. in the dis-guised Shakespearian handwriting, he came across a line which caused him to exclaim to Mr. Ireland: "This is rather strange, for though you are ac-quainted with my opinion as to Shakespeare, yet, be it as it may, he certainly always wrote poetry". Further on he commented as follows: "There are certainly some bold ideas, but they are crude and undigested. It is very odd; one would be led to think that Shakespeare must have been very young when he wrote the play. As to the doubting whether it be really his or not, who can possibly look at the papers, and not believe them ancient?" Yet Malone, the eminent critic, had convinced Kemble, the actor, that the play was spurious, and in his *Inquiry into the Authenticity of Certain Miscel-laneous Papers*, published within a few days of the first and last performance of "Vortigern," accounted quite correctly for the antiquity of the actual paper, which is said to have made such an impression on Sheridan: "The true and natural paper-warehouse for such a schemer to repair to is the shop of a book-seller, where every folio and quarto of the age of Elizabeth and James would supply a couple of single leaves of white-brown paper, of the hue required" (311). As Malone had been from the first an active disbeliever in all the Shakespearian forgeries of which "Vortigern" was only the last, Sheridan can hardly

15 *

have been really deceived by the antiquity of the paper, and Kemble's story goes to indicate that he was more deceiving than deceived. Kemble, despite his own scepticism, consented to act in the play, in deference to Sheridan's request, who "thought it would be good for the treasury"! "You know very well," he said to Kemble, "that an Englishman considers himself as good a judge of Shakespeare as of his pint of porter" (*Clubs of London*, ii., 107).

And how did the Englishman judge his Shakespeare? Did he agree with the critics who declared that "Vortigern," though inferior to Shakespeare's best plays, was superior to his worst? There are several accounts of the momentous night, but though they differ considerably in detail they all agree that the play was most irretrievably and conclusively damned.

According to the *Times* of the following Monday the first Act was fairly heard, though every line of it "spoke itself an actual forgery". The second and third Acts proved less tolerable, whilst the fourth elicited "rude murmurs" and "continual merriment," whilst in the fifth Act the speech on Death, "on which the great hope of the authenticity" of the play rested, drew down bursts of laughter, which reached its culmination when Kemble delivered the words—

"I would this solemn mockery were o'er".

This account agrees in the main with that given by young Ireland in his *Confessions* (1805). But a very different account is attributed to Kemble by the author (possibly William Marsh, M.P.) of *The Clubs of London* (ii., 107).

According to Kemble, the first Act, much of the second, and a few speeches in the third were "endured". There were occasional deep growls of disapprobation, but they were silenced for a time by Humphry Sturt, who roared out from the stage box "with the intonation of a bull" to "give the thing a fair trial". When Kemble reached the fatal line, "the most overwhelming sounds of mingled groans and laughter ran through the house," though for a few moments the brazen voice of Sturt again secured silence. But when Phillimore called out to the soldiers who were carrying off Rowena, " Give her up, give her up, oh, give her up," the same Humphry "threw himself back on the bench and burst into a fit of horse-laughing as deafening as the falls of Niagara, and the rest of the audience caught the infection. 'Give her up, give her up,' resounded from a thousand tongues. The hint was taken and the curtain fell."

But the words do not occur in the extant editions of "Vortigern". Kemble himself played the part of Vortigern, and must as Vortigern have spoken the line about the solemn mockery; yet in this interview he is made to say that it was as Vortigern that Phillimore called out to the soldiers to give up Rowena. But Phillimore's name is attached to the part of Horsus in the playbill, and Ireland says that it was the dying of Phillimore as Horsus in fight with Pascentius in the fourth scene of the fourth Act that gave a "deadly blow" to his play. For Phillimore managed to fall with the drop-curtain across his body, his feet facing the audience, and there he lay groaning under its weight for some moments till, though dead, he extricated himself, to the great amusement of the spectators. Phillimore was famous for the size of his nose, and Ireland, the elder, never forgave him for his acting on this occasion; the length of his nose, he said, was "enough to damn the finest play Shakespeare ever wrote".

Nor did he forgive Kemble, who, when he came to the already quoted line, uttered it "in the most sepulchral tone of voice possible," whereupon "the most discordant howl echoed from the pit that ever assailed the organs of hearing, and continued for ten minutes," when Kemble, "in order to amuse the audience still more, redelivered the very line above quoted with even more solemn grimace than he had in the first instance displayed".

So says young Ireland in his *Confessions*, published in 1805, and his account was corroborated by an eye-witness who as "Octogenarian" gave his re-collections of the event sixty-one years later in *Notes and Queries* (20th June, 1857). But Octogenarian's memory was given in correction of that of another eye-witness who had said in the number for 6th June of the same periodical that when Kemble came to the words, "Then catch him by the throat," he grasped his throat "with a rather ludicrous action" and paused, when "a slight laugh arose, and he himself appeared to be struggling with convulsive laughter, and then burst out a roar of genuine mirth from the pit, which was taken up by the whole house. From that moment the condemnation was complete, and the termination was accompanied by the same roars of laughter as attend the broadest farce ever exhibited upon the English stage." But the recited words are not in the existing versions of the play, where the allusion is to the feet, not the throat; so that the only conclusion can be that the writer had slightly forgotten the facts, though as to the actual fate of the play all writers are agreed.

One can imagine meantime the misery of poor Samuel Ireland, the father, a firm believer in the genuineness of the play fabricated by his son, as he sat with his friends in a central box, and watched the impression it produced. He would have nothing to do with the prologue written by Pye, the poet-laureate; he required the stronger committal vouch-safed by Sir James Burgess, who prefaced the play with a prologue which concluded as follows :—

From deep oblivion snatched, this play appears :
It claims respect, since Shakespeare's name it bears ;
That name, the source of wonder and delight,
To a fair hearing has at least a right.
We ask no more—with you the judgment lies ;
No forgeries escape your piercing eyes !
Unbiass'd then pronounce your dread decree,
Alike from prejudice and favour free.

If, the fierce ordeal pass'd, you chance to find
Rich sterling ore, tho' rude and unrefined,
Stamp it your own ; assert your poet's fame,
And add fresh wreaths to Shakespeare's honoured name.

And what of the feelings of the son, the juvenile author of all this commotion? No wonder he soon left the paternal box, and disappeared behind the scenes, where at the beginning of the third Act Mrs. Jordan congratulated him on its probable success. And one can almost believe him when he says that after it was all over he "retired to bed, more easy in mind than he had been for a great length of time, as the load was removed which had oppressed him". That night he slept "most profoundly"—as befits the happy age of eighteen.

The magnificence of the hoax, its extreme cleverness, its close approximation to success, might have entitled the youthful culprit to more lenient treatment than he received.

He was driven from the solicitor's office in New Inn where all his forgeries had been concocted, and the home in Norfolk Street knew him no more. The moralist may decree that justice was meted out to him, but what casuist shall fairly apportion their proper shares of blame between the youth who forged the play, the proprietor who accepted it despite abundant reasons for believing it to be forged, and the great manager-actor who firmly believing it to be forged played his part with the apparent design of ruining its success as a play?

But if this charge can fairly be laid against Kemble, at least posterity owes him some gratitude. For what if the play had succeeded, as Ireland always thought it might have done, had it only been acted at Covent Garden, whither the King and Court were wont to resort? All chance of success was averted by Kemble's acting, and by Malone's famous *Inquiry*. This work had been published, according to the *Times*, shortly before the eventful night, and the purport of it was conveyed to the public by handbills freely distributed on the day of the representation. The *Times*, like Ireland, the father, blamed Malone for striking just at the critical moment; " We cannot help observing," it said, with its familiar unctuous rectitude, "that Mr. Malone's publication against the authenticity of the play only two days before it was to be represented was a very unfair proceeding and extremely illiberal ". Yet Malone had only had three months in which to complete a work of over 400 pages, and what could he do better than denounce a forgery at the very moment when it was possible it might befool the public?

Had the result been otherwise, young Ireland was ready to flood the world with other plays of Shakespeare.

In ten weeks he wrote the play of " Henry II.," which he gave in his own handwriting to his father, from the supposed original MS., which he intended to produce on old paper in the disguised handwriting, had not the failure of "Vortigern" led to the confession of the whole story. "Henry II.," a decided improvement on "Vortigern," was in its turn to have been followed by a series of plays covering all the reigns between William I. and Elizabeth, and all were to have been attributed to Shakespeare! And the father enumerated a long list of portions of plays and other writings of Shakespeare, including a brief autobiography, which this promising lad swore that he had seen and doubtless would have produced. To what confusion might not all this have led but for Kemble and Malone, and to what disquieting reflections does it not give rise touching the comparative facility of forgery?

The only person connected with "Vortigern" who came morally well out of it was Samuel Ireland, the father, though it was not till long after his death in 1800 that his memory was finally cleared of complicity in the fraud.

In 1876 his literary remains were bought from his nephew by the British Museum, and they placed his innocence beyond all doubt. In November, 1796, he published his *Vindication*, explaining his conduct in the matter. It is clear from the preface that, though the main facts were then admitted, he still doubted whether the Shakespearian relics were really spurious or genuine. He disbelieved all his son's confessions, from sheer inability, so natural in a father, to credit him with the capacity to produce such works. His son's declarations about the source of the papers had been made to him " in the most solemn and awful manner before crowds of the most eminent characters" who came to his house, and he could not therefore have cherished the slightest suspicion of his veracity. His story, too, had been corroborated in the most solemn manner by his son's friend and confidant, Montague Talbot, in several letters ; the *Vindication* in short bore all the marks of plausibility and truth.

But it failed to carry conviction. The *a priori* improbability of a mere youth accomplishing such a fraud deprived it of credit. Ritson, the antiquary, in a letter about it to Laing, the bookseller, wrote : " All the plays, deeds, letters and papers of every description which have been produced by Ireland owe their existence solely to his son Samuel, alias William Henry, a boy of nineteen, in whom no talents of any kind were ever before discovered even by the father himself, who has in fact been the completest of all possible dupes to the astonishing artifices of this second Chatterton " (1st Dec., 1796, Nichol's *Lit. Ill.*, iii., 779).

But others were not so believing as Ritson. The famous George Steevens in a letter to Bishop Percy, dated 26th December, 1796, declared that the *Vindication* exhibited " fresh indications of forgery ". As to the son's *Authentic Account of the Shakespearian Manuscripts*, in which he had done his best to exonerate his father from all guilt in the matter, that was merely " a new game of fraud," and " produced with the sole view of whitewashing the senior culprit"; the quarrel between father and son was only simulated (Nichol's *Lit. Ill.*, vii., 9).

This was the story that despite young Ireland's *Confessions*, published in 1805, prevailed for about eighty years. Dr. Ingleby, writing in 1859, declared that the father "was the general who devised and methodised the strategy, and executed the simulated handwriting; W. H. Ireland's duty was merely that of amanuensis and copier for his excellent parent. . . . The house of the Irelands was in fact a manufactory of forgeries, done for the sole object of making money" (*Shakespearian Fabrications*, 100). And Mr. Fitzgerald, in his book on the Kembles, in 1871, wrote of the "bold imposture of 'Vortigern' put forward by the *Irelands*" (i., 338). But this view was entirely erroneous, as Dr. Ingleby himself candidly admitted in his "Literary Career of a Shakespeare Forger," appended to his work on Shakespeare published in 1877, after he had inspected the papers of Samuel Ireland, then recently acquired by the British Museum: "My own examination of these voluminous papers has removed from my mind all doubt as to the complete exculpation of the old man".

But it remains hard on the old man that he should have died under the suspicion of forgery, and perhaps by reason of it, and then had to wait all those years for his memory to be cleared of the aspersions of critics who had no justifiable data for their judgment. Time in this case has amply verified the vain efforts made by the son to excul- pate his father, and the general credibility of his *Confessions* has been undoubtedly enhanced by their proved veracity on this single point. The worst that can be said against the father is that he was too enthusiastic about Shakespeare : he talked about him daily, and read his works constantly in the family circle, doubtless to that circle's weariness. But dearly did he pay for it, for it rendered him the natural and easy prey of imposition, and one can almost believe the statement of William Henry that it was to please rather than to deceive his parent, that he executed his first forgery, the autograph of Shakespeare ap- pended to the supposed lease from himself and Heminge to Michael Fraser and his wife.

The success of this attempt led to the concoction of all those other forgeries which made the year 1795 so memorable in literary annals. It would be tedious to dwell in detail on all the legal documents, re- ceipts and so forth signed by Shakespeare, which in rapid succession issued from the office in New Inn. They can still be studied in the *Miscellaneous Papers and Legal Instruments under the hand and seal of William Shakespeare*, published by Samuel Ireland, their proud possessor, in 1796.

This publication the son naturally opposed as long as he could. So long as they could only be seen in Norfolk Street, there was hope of escape from detection, but, once let them be printed, they would lie at the mercy of Malone. And it was little mercy Malone showed them after they were published. His *Inquiry*, published the following April, may have been of needless length, but it was a triumphant piece of criticism, and it was at once and for ever fatal. Many of the words in the MSS. were not in use in the sixteenth century, and the weird spelling belonged to no known age of English letters.

And in justification of the length of Malone's criticism it must be remembered that a belief in the papers had begun to take no small hold of public opinion.

Samuel Ireland's own too simple faith infected others, who came in crowds to see the precious relics at Norfolk Street. It is true that Ritson came, and after a few pointed questions went away without a word, leaving no doubt as to his real verdict, and that Porson, when asked to attest his belief in the papers, said that he made a point of never subscribing to confessions of faith; but many men of no mean fame readily signed what Steevens afterwards called "that register of shame," the elder Ireland's lists of believers in the papers. Of these the first was signed on 25th February, 1795, and the second in March of the following year, when "Vortigern," "Lear," and the deed in favour of Ireland had been added to the earlier collection. The idea of such a testimonial seems to have originated with Boswell, who saw them within a few months of his death (19th May, 1795). He examined first the documents themselves, and then their language in the fair copies that had been made from the disguised handwritings. His labours compelled him to call for a tumbler of warm brandy and water. After that he redoubled his praises of the MSS., and declared that he should now die happy, having lived to see such a day. Finally he knelt before the volume and exclaimed : " I now kiss the invaluable relics of our bard, and thanks to God that I have lived to see them ". Such is young Ireland's story, which is confirmed by that given by his father in his *Vindication*. It must be set on the credit side of these absurd forgeries that they thus helped to cheer the last days of the amiable and eminent biographer.

The learned Dr. Parr was in favour of a stronger testimonial than that suggested by Boswell, and it was finally couched in the following terms :—

" We, whose names are hereunto subscribed, have in the presence of and by favour of Mr. Ireland inspected the Shakespeare papers, and are convinced of their authenticity ". Among the twenty-one names are those of Parr himself, of Boswell, of Pinkerton, of three peers (Somerset, Lauderdale and Kinnaird), and of Pye, the poet-laureate. Some of the names on this first list are the same which appear on the list of a year later, but several are different. By that time faith in " Lear " and " Vortigern " required to be added to faith in the previous discoveries, and in the interval perhaps doubts had arisen. The father

deemed the supposed find of the original of " Lear " a
" national discovery," and accepted as improvements
all the alterations of the text which his son had
made in his new original edition. He regretted that
only a portion of the original of " Hamlet " had been
discovered. But would he, as a supposed party to
the fraud, have informed his readers of so suspicious
a fact as that on the paper of the " Lear " MS. more
than twenty different water-marks were discernible?

Among the earlier forgeries was Shakespeare's
" Profession of Faith," which young Ireland says that
he wrote off just as the thoughts arose in his mind
" without any previous transcript or subsequent
alteration ". When the secret came out, it seemed
absurd enough that Shakespeare should have concluded his long effusion with such words as these
(in modern spelling) :—

" O cherish us like the sweet chicken that under
the cover of her spreading wings receives her little
brood and hovering over them keeps them harmless
and in safety ".

But at the time this " Profession " was much ad-
mired. When the father read it out to Dr. Parr and
Dr. Joseph Wharton, one of them, probably the latter,
exclaimed : " Sir, we have very fine passages in our
Church Service, and our litany abounds with beauties,
but here, Sir, is a man who has distanced us all ".
Yet Dr. J. Wharton's name is absent from the list
of the believers. But it was the encouragement thus
given by his fatal praise which tempted Ireland to

further efforts, the " Profession " being the first forgery in which he had ventured beyond the simple auto-graph of Shakespeare's name.

Mr. F. Webb, who signed both the testimonials and who was a man of letters and learning, was so convinced of the genuineness of the forgeries that under the title of " Philalethes " he published a pamphlet in their defence.   He wrote : " I am fully satisfied and believe that no human wisdom, cunning, art, or deceit, if they could be united, are equal to the task of such an imposture ".   Again : " What man or set of men who had sat down with an intention to deceive the world by palming upon it forgeries of plays in the name of Shakespeare could possibly have deemed it necessary to the support of such a design to have fabricated such writings and forged such legal instruments as those which now exist ? "   A perfectly fair and unanswerable argument, and often urged on behalf of other works than Ireland's ; and yet how perfectly wrong! Of Shakespeare's addresses to Ann Hathaway he writes : " Nature and Nature alone produces documents like these.   They are marked with the authentic seal of her artless simplicity. These are fine touches, which imposture can never imitate."

And these are the verses :—

> Is there in heaven aught more rare
> Than thou sweet nymph of Avon fair
> Is there on earth a man more true
> Than Willy Shakespeare is to you

16

Though fickle fortune prove unkind
Still doth she leave her wealth behind
She ne'er the heart can form anew
Nor make thy Willy's love untrue

Though age with withered hand do strike
The form most fair the face most bright
Still doth she leave untouched and true
Thy Willy's love and friendship too

Though death with never failing blow
Doth man and babe alike bring low
Yet doth he take naught but his due
And strikes not Willy's heart still true

Since then nor fortune death nor age
Can faithful Willy's love assuage
Then do I live and die for you
Thy Willy sincere and most true.

The other sample of Nature's work ran as follows :—

"DEAREST ANNA,

"As thou hast always found me to my word most true so thou shalt see I have strictly kept my promise I pray you perfume this my little lock with thy balmy eyes so then indeed shall kings themselves bow and pay homage to it I do assure thee no rude hand hath knotted it thy Willie's alone hath done the work. Neither the gilded bauble that environs the head of Majesty no nor honours most weighty would give me half the joy as did this my little work for thee. The feeling that did nearest approach unto it was that which cometh nighest unto

God meek and gentle charity for that virtue o Anna
do I love thee do I cherish thee into my heart for
thou art as a tall cedar stretching forth its branches
and succouring smaller plants from nipping winter or
-the boisterous winds. Farewell tomorrow by times
I will see thee till then Adieu sweet love.

>   " Thine ever,
>
>   " WM. SHAKESPEARE."

The feelings of Webb, Chalmers, and other
believers, when the fraud was confessed, can better
be imagined than described. But however impossible they found it to forgive the author of all their
deception, for posterity it has its amusing side. No
better farce has ever been enacted on the stage of
real life. For these compositions must have been
pored over and pronounced genuine by all who signed
the first testimonial. They caused Boswell to burst
into a kind of *Nunc dimittis*, and were perhaps ad-
mired as inimitable productions by Pye, the poet-
laureate, of whom Sir Walter Scott so cruelly said
that in everything but his poetry he was eminently
respectable.

The faith of the elder Ireland was, therefore, only
coincident with that of more competent judges than
himself. His credulity was no more reprehensible
than theirs. What more could he have done to test
the value of the documents than he did by the
publicity he gave them? He not only courted the
criticism of the learned, but facilitated their inquiries

16 *

by having the illegible originals transcribed into
modern handwriting.   And then he published them
for the inspection of the whole world.   There had
been, as he truly said in the preface to this publication of the *Miscellaneous Papers*, "no disinterested
individual, in the circle of literature, to whose critical
eye he had not been earnest that the whole should be
subjected.   He had courted, he had even challenged,
the critical judgment of those who were best skilled
in the poetry and phraseology in which Shakespeare
lived : as well as those, whose profession or course of
study had made them conversant with ancient deeds,
writings, seals and autographs."   The paper-maker
as well as the professional author had been taken
into counsel.   He argued fairly that it was impossible,
amidst so many various sources of detection, for a
forger to have escaped detection.   As to the charge
against himself of imposing on the public, "no consideration" would have tempted him to such a fraud ;
"had even the possibility of forging these papers
been in his estimation within the reach of art, they
should never have met the public eye".   No wonder
that, when at last the letter came from his son, a boy
of eighteen, confessing his fraud, the father received
it with frank disbelief.   Not only no single man, but
no set of men, could, he argued, have produced the
mass of evidence then in his possession ; he still
believed they were Shakespeare's ; the idea of their
being his son's work was quite inadmissible.

One almost wonders how his reason survived the

ultimate acceptance of the truth. For nearly two years the poor bookseller had been one of the most famous men in England; the highest and most learned in the land had visited him in Norfolk Street; the Prince of Wales himself had carefully scrutinised the relics. Think of all those to whom, as to the prince, he had read that wondrous passage about the "sweet chicken"; think of those to whom he had shown with pride in its gilt casket that most precious relic of Shakespeare's hair, or of those to whom rings had been given with small cuttings from these precious locks. Think of the contemplated new Life of Shakespeare, destined to throw a new light upon his character; the book from Shakespeare's library, with the poet's own annotations, displaying "a disposition amiable and gentle as his genius was transcendent"; the "Profession of Faith," proving the poet to have been a Protestant; the letter to Cowley, the actor, with its "witty conundrum," proving him to have been so good-natured and playful. Think of all these dreams dispelled, this burst of glory over, and the whole thing admitted to have been a sordid and heartless forgery practised upon him by his own son, a mere lad of eighteen! The limits of a father's forgiveness should not be straitened, but the strain on Samuel Ireland's powers was unusually severe, nor can we be surprised that he failed under it.

Neither at home, therefore, nor in the world was any forgiveness possible for so stupendous a hoax.

Young Ireland survived his confession some forty years, dying finally in 1835. In 1832 he reprinted "Vortigern" with an account of its history. And he produced certain novels to which his earlier history lends a kind of interest.

But he fell short of the early promise which he gave under the borrowed plumes of Shakespeare. For when all is said, both "Vortigern" and "Henry II." remain extraordinary literary feats for a boy to have accomplished. It would seem that the mere effort of writing after an assumed model acts as a kind of hypnotic self-suggestion, and renders the intellect capable of otherwise impossible performance. For neither of these plays could or would have been written but for the hope and prospect, which gradually unfolded itself, of palming them off on the world as the works of Shakespeare.

Ireland admits the influence which the story of Chatterton exercised on his own career. He used frequently, he says, to envy his fate, and desire nothing so ardently as the termination of his own existence in a similar cause. Allowance must be made for the period in which his life was cast ; for it was a kind of golden age of forgery. He himself paid the full penalty of his offence, but others of his contemporaries, without the excuse of youth, seem to have suffered little loss of reputation for their detected and admitted deceptions.

What are we to say, for instance, of George Steevens, the eminent critic of Shakespeare and the malevolent enemy of the elder Ireland, whom Disraeli described as "a creature so spotted over with literary forgeries and adulterations that any remarkable one about the time he flourished may be attributed to him"? He it was who originated the story of the upas-tree of Java; who deceived Gough, the antiquarian, by a fabricated stone inscribed with the name of Hardiknute; and who forged an account in the *Theatrical Mirror* of a "merry meeting at the Globe" between Shakespeare and Ben Jonson and Ned Alleyne, in a letter purporting to have been written by George Peele, the actor, and dated 1600, two years after that actor is known to have been dead, though there is no certain knowledge of the actual date of his death (*Curiosities of Literature*, vi., 78). But what penalty did he, who was so bitter against Ireland, pay for his own incursions into the same forbidden land?

The story of the Ireland forgeries raises several reflections. For here were documents fabricated by a mere boy, of no special learning or education, and, instead of being in any way concealed, exposed most openly to publicity and criticism; yet in an age of learning they deceived many of the very elect of the learned world. What then may not have been possible in the line of forgery in the times when a forger had no publicity, no scrutiny, no printed version of his fabrications to reckon with? The possibilities were simply limitless, and almost justify the scepticism of Hardouin, the Jesuit, who held that most of the Greek and Latin classics were the works of the monks in the middle ages.　Such scepticism would undoubtedly be too far-reaching, but it is hardly inadmissible on the score of an apparent absence of motive.　The mere amusement of a hoax upon his father, and men of learning generally, appears to have been young Ireland's primary or only motive.　Yet the apparent absence of motive was one of the chief arguments in favour of the documents adduced by believers in them.　What motive, they asked, could a forger have had in producing documents of such variety, exposing himself to fresh risk of detection in every one he added to their number ; and what did it conduce to the palming off as Shakespeare's of his own edition of " King Lear " to forge such a document as the Deed of Trust to John Hemynge ?　Would a forger have cast such imputations on Shakespeare's character as are cast on it in that deed ?　All these arguments were as justifiable as they are familiar, yet they were all erroneous. And how many arguments based on *a priori* speculations of the probable or improbable workings of a forger's mind, like those, for instance, in such a work as Paley's *Horæ Paulinæ*, are discredited by the literary controversy that raged round these Shakespearian forgeries ?

Questions of style and spelling apart, the believers in the forgeries had a stronger main argument than their opponents : it was far more likely that the papers were genuine than that any individual could have had time or motive sufficient to forge them. Yet they were forged in a very short time, by a very simple process, and by a youth of no experience in literature. If ever there was an incident calculated to inspire learning with a perception of the wisdom of sobriety and modesty of judgment in matters literary, and of an absence of dogmatism, it was the case of the lad in the lawyer's office who for his own sport carried such unspeakable havoc into the camp of the learned.

CHAPTER XV.

AMONG THE BALLAD FORGERS.

There are few books to which the world owes more pleasure than it does to John Pinkerton's *Collection of the best and most Interesting Voyages and Travels in all Parts of the World*, which was first published in 1808, when the collector was in his fiftieth year. He also enlightened the world on the subject of medals and Scotch history, and amused it by his unwearied declamations on the inferiority of the Celt.

But he, too, had, at least in his earlier days, no scruple about deceiving the world, and has in consequence his place amongst the forgers of literature. He was only eighteen when he set to work on the ballad of "Hardyknute," which he edited with a second part in 1781 together with twenty-one other *Scottish Tragic Ballads*. Two years later he published a second edition with a second volume of *Comic Ballads*.

But the second year, Ritson, the antiquary, appeared on the scene, in a somewhat fiery temper. In a letter in the *Gentleman's Magazine* (November, 1874) he proclaimed the forgery of some of these ballads. "Your success," he writes, addressing Pinkerton, "has doubtless fully gratified your expectations, and the dexterity of a pickpocket may vie with the impudence of a highwayman." Ritson elsewhere declares that "the history of Scottish poetry exhibits a series of fraud, forgery and imposture, practised with impunity and success," and that "the forgeries of Hector Boethius, David Chalmers, George Buchanan, Thomas Dempster, Sir John Bruce, William Lauder, James Macpherson, and John Pinkerton, stamp a disgrace upon the national character, which ages of exceptional integrity will be required to remove" (*Historical Essay on Scottish Song*, 63).

Ritson at all events prevented Pinkerton from forging any more Scotch poetry with either impunity or success. The letter in the *Gentleman's Magazine* can have been no soft punishment, and with it went all hope in that direction. Pinkerton claimed to have given the ballad of "Hardyknute" "in its original perfection"; it was "certainly the most noble production in this style that ever appeared in the world". For the recovered stanzas he was indebted "to the memory of a lady in Lanarkshire".

In reality "Hardyknute" was of no older date than 1719, when it first appeared at Edinburgh as a fragment in a small folio. In his Preface to *Ancient Scottish Poems*, published in 1786, Pinkerton declared that he really believed in the antiquity of the first part of the ballad; as to the second part "the editor must now confess himself guilty," and he craved the pardon of his friends and of the public.

With regard to other ballads which Ritson had also denounced as forgeries in his collection, " The Laird of Woodhouselie," " Lord Livingstone," " Binnorie," " The Death of Monteith," and " I wish I were where Helen lies," all purporting to have been collected from tradition, the real and then youthful author wrote as follows : " Since the editor of these volumes is in the confessional he must not omit that in the first volume, besides the second part of ' Hardyknute,' No. 16, ' The Laird of Woodhouselie,' is written by him, as is No. 17, ' Lord Livingstone,' yet of both he had small lines from tradition. No. 13, ' Binnorie,' is one-half from tradition, one-half by the editor, though he could not now himself distinguish the lines. No. 19, ' Death of Monteith,' is wholly by the editor, upon no tradition whatever. . . . No. 21, ' I wish I were where Helen lies,' is all the editor's ; save the three first lines, which he heard a lady repeat."

Ritson therefore had been perfectly justified in saying of this little volume of *Tragic Ballads* that its most prominent feature was "the studied and systematic forgery" that pervaded the whole. This he said in 1794, when he published two small volumes of *Scottish Songs* of his own collecting. In the meantime in 1786 Pinkerton, pleading his youth and his desire to please the public in extenuation of his earlier fraud, had brought out his two volumes of

Ancient Scottish Poems from the MS. collections of Sir Richard Maitland in the Pepysian Library at Cambridge. It is hardly to be wondered at that this second publication aroused much suspicion, and that Pinkerton's detailed account of the Maitland MSS. was by some regarded as a fabrication. Chambers in his *Biographical Dictionary of Eminent Scotchmen* declared that "this forgery was one of the most audacious in the annals of transcribing". But for this charge there was no justification; Pinkerton this time treated the reading public honestly, and the MSS. in question may be seen at Cambridge to this very day.

Pinkerton enjoyed some revenge over Ritson, when the latter published his collection of Scottish songs in 1794, for in the *Scots Magazine* he availed himself to the full of the privilege of the man whose enemy has had the indiscretion to write a book. Yet the verdict of posterity must be on the side of Ritson, but for whose sagacity and intervention the younger author might have been tempted to still further and more extensive experiments upon public credulity. It was Ritson who elicited the ultimate confession of deception, and to whom the cause of the purity of letters must always remain indebted for his detection of a shameless attempt at deception and for his timely and salutary castigation of the deceiver.

The great master of ballad lore, Sir Walter Scott, had no sympathy with the noble rage of Ritson against ballad-forgers. He wrote, in April, 1830:

"There is no small degree of cant in the violent invectives with which impostors of this nature have been assailed. If a young author wishes to circulate a beautiful poem under the guise of antiquity, the public is surely more enriched by the contribution than injured by the deception." He adds that "it is hardly possible to succeed in deceiving those who have made this branch of literature their study". But the forgery of a ballad, "as it must rest on deception, cannot be altogether honourable" (*Border Minstrelsy*, 1833, i., 16, 17).

Sir Walter, as is said later, was himself taken in by several ballads forged by Surtees of Mainsforth. But had he been undeceived, he would only have laughed, though Surtees' part in the affair "was hardly an honourable one". Scott was a lover of poetry first, antiquarianism was only a good second in his affections. There is a legend about a novelist who induced a divine to advertise a pious romance of his, and being a light-hearted person, cried, "I have spoofed the old boy first shot". Was Sir Walter, as a ballad collector, spoofed first shot by James Hogg, the Ettrick Shepherd? Was the ballad of "Auld Maitland," obtained from oral recitation by Scott just after the publication of the first edition of his *Border Minstrelsy* (spring of 1802), a concoction by James Hogg? "A hoax was to Hogg as the breath of his nostrils," says Lockhart, but did Hogg hoax Scott in 1802 with "Auld Maitland"? Is the ballad a forgery?

Here we must enter into details.   Professor
Child does not print "Auld Maitland" in his vast
collection of ballads.   In the small early edition of
1861, he is "inclined to agree with Aytoun that this
ballad is a modern imitation, or, if not that, of com-
paratively recent composition".   Rather curiously
Scott gives two different accounts of how he obtained
the ballad.   Writing to Ellis in the autumn of 1802
he says that he and Leyden were much surprised
when the ballad "was presented to us copied down
from the recitation of an old shepherd by a country
farmer," who, almost certainly, was Will Laidlaw,
later Scott's friend, steward and amanuensis (Lockhart's *Scott*, ii., 99, 100).   In the *Border Minstrelsy*
Scott gives the ballad as "written down from the
recitation of the mother of James Hogg, who sings,
or rather chaunts it, with great animation.   She
learned the ballad from a blind man who died at
the advanced age of ninety."   Hogg's "Lines to Sir
W. Scott" give a vivid picture of the effect on the
poet of his mother's recitation :—

> "When Maitland's song first met your ear,
> How the furled visage up did clear,
> Beaming delight ! though now a shade
> Of doubt would darken into dread
> That some unskilled presumptious arm
> Had marred tradition's mighty charm.
>   Scarce grew thy lurking dread the less,
> Till she, the ancient minstreless,
> With fervid voice, and kindling eye,
> And withered arms waving on high,

Sang forth these words in eldritch shriek,
While tears stood on thy nut-brown cheek—

> ‘Na, we are nane o’ the lads o’ France,
>   Nor e’er pretend to be ;
> We be three lads of fair Scotland,
>   Auld Maitland’s sons, a’ three ! ’

Thy fist made all the table ring—
‘ By ——, sir, but that is the thing ’.”

Now the blind man seems to have been either
the shepherd from whose recitation the farmer had
taken a written copy, or, more probably, the shepherd was of the Laidlaw clan, namely, Will of Phau-
hope, an uncle of Hogg’s, who, to his nephew’s
disgust, deserted minstrelsy for the works of the
early leaders of the Secession, such as the Rev.
Ralph Erskine (*Letters of Sir W. Scott*, i., 12, 13).
Hogg’s account, in *Domestic Manners of Sir Walter
Scott* (1838), is that his mother recited the ballad to
Scott, and that the original source, as far as she
knew, was Auld Barbara Maitland, the housekeeper
of “the first laird of Tushielaw”. She must have
meant the first of the Anderson lairds, who succeeded
the ancient Scott lairds of Tushielaw. It thus appears that both the aged shepherd and Mrs. Hogg
knew the ballad, and it is highly improbable that
James Hogg first forged it and then made old people
learn the long ballad by rote, “and the same with
intent to deceive”. The ballad is about “ Maitland
upon auld bierd grey,” celebrated by Gawain Douglas
(about 1510-1520) in a list of heroes of romance.

And in the Maitland MSS. of about 1570 there is a reference to Auld Sir Richard Maitland,

> his auld baird grey
> And to his noble sonnes three,

the three sons who are the heroes of the ballad, and enemies to King Edward of England. About the ballad Hogg wrote to Scott, saying that it was no forgery; "the contrary will be proved by most of the old people hereabouts having a great part of it by heart".

There is in the Maitland MSS. any amount of proof that, in 1570-1580, Auld Maitland and his three sons were famous characters of old romance. Only from the MSS. themselves, or from Pinkerton's version of them in his *Ancient Scottish Poems* of 1792, could Hogg have known the fundamental facts of the ballad. Enjoying as he did the free run of William Laidlaw's book-shelves, and being a subscriber to the library at Peebles, it is possible that in this way he became acquainted with Pinkerton's reproductions of those ancient poems.

Hogg, therefore, if he was the forger, based the ballad on Pinkerton's edition of the Maitland MSS., adding in brackets four lines of his own, to fill up the sense of two half-forgotten verses; an artful mode of deception also adopted by Surtees. He threw in obsolete words like "sowies" and "springalds" (pronounced "spring walls" by the reciter) and "portcullize," and he, probably, introduced a note on various readings by "some reciters". If Scott wrote

17

this note, Scott had heard *several* reciters. The obsolete words Hogg might have found in Blind Harry's poem of " Wallace," a great favourite of the Scottish peasantry.

Such then was the unequalled astuteness of Hogg, if so early as 1802 and so unversed in literature as he then was, he forged the ballad, and induced old people to learn it by heart and recite it. The whole trick seems impossible, and the knowledge of the ballad by old people appears to indicate that it is a traditional survival from, perhaps, the sixteenth century, when, as we know, Auld Maitland and his three sons were familiar heroes of romance or poetry. Let us add that Hogg never boasted of " hoaxing the Shirra " with this ballad, even after the Shirra was dead. He still told the same story of his mother's recitation of the piece in his *Domestic Manners of Sir Walter Scott*. But when the Shepherd had taken in Jeffrey with a "faked" Jacobite song, he crowed aloud like chanticleer in his glee. For these reasons it seems that Professor Child was too sceptical when he wholly rejected " Auld Maitland ". Old Barbara Maitland, quoted by Hogg as his mother's source, may well have known a ballad about the glories of her family.

In the matter of ballad-forging, Pinkerton was far from standing alone. Strange in this respect was the imposition practised on Sir Walter Scott by Robert Surtees, the celebrated antiquary and historian of the County of Durham, who not only

palmed off on Sir Walter as antique three ballads
purely of his own composition, but actually suffered
them to occupy a place in the *Minstrelsy of the
Scottish Border*, with a fictitious account of their
origin, and left him deceived to the end of his days.

The "Death of Featherstonhaugh," supposed to
relate an incident in the clan feuds of the Ridleys and
the Featherstones, was represented to be an "old
Northumbrian ballad". The novelist tells us in his
innocence that "it was taken down from the recitation of an old woman eighty years of age, mother of
one of the miners in Alston-moor, by the agent of the
lead mines there, who communicated it to my friend,
R. Surtees, Esq. of Mainsforth. She had not, she
said, heard it for many years ; but, when she was a
girl, it used to be sung at merry-makings, till the roof
rang again."

Sir Walter never suspected these old women of
his friend Surtees. It was another old woman, Anne
Douglas, who weeded in Surtees' garden, from whom
Surtees obtained the "beautiful fragment" called
"Bartram's Dirge". In this case the real composer
inserted within brackets certain words and lines which
he professed to have added to certain defective stanzas,
thereby naturally averting all suspicion that all the
eight stanzas of the poem were entirely his own.
Could deception have been more subtle?

And yet a third song, called "Lord Ewrie," also
of eight stanzas, was included by Sir Walter in
his collection. It was, he says, "written down by

17 *

my obliging friend, Robert Surtees, Esq. of Mainsforth, from the recitation of Rose Smith, of Bishop
Middleham, a woman aged upwards of ninety-one,
whose husband's father and two brothers were killed
in the affair of 1715 ".   But here again the old woman
was Surtees himself, he being the sole author of the
poem.   To a man like Surtees, in whose honour the
Surtees Society was founded, much no doubt may
fairly claim to be forgiven, and the fraud he practised
on Sir Walter would possibly have been condoned
by that good-humoured victim.   Still, Surtees' conception of the duties of friendship strikes one as
singular.

 And the ease with which Sir Walter was deceived
in these three cases reflects seriously on his trust-
worthiness as a guide with regard to the antiquity of
other ballads collected in his *Minstrelsy*.   In no line
of literature has forgery found an easier field than in
that of ancient ballads : the pleasure and ease of
deceiving the learned being doubtless the primary
motive.   Thus Lady Wardlaw was the real authoress
in 1719 of the famous ballad of " Hardyknute,"
which she pretended to have found written on shreds
of old paper ; and her hand has been suspected in
certain other ballads that pass for ancient.

 In the nineteenth century the Rev. R. S. Hawker
"was amused" to see his ballad, "Sir Beville," inserted in a collection of old ballads ; whilst his ballad
of " Trelawney" was not only accepted as genuine
by Scott, Macaulay and Dickens, but in 1846 it was

printed in Mr. Dixon's *Ancient Poems, Ballads, Songs of the Peasantry of England, taken down from Oral Tradition,* published by the Percy Society in 1832. Yet Hawker had avowed himself its author in the year 1825!

The Surtees' forgeries make a bad story, but a case of even worse forgery, though of better poetry, is afforded by the fraud practised by Allan Cunningham on Mr. Cromek in 1809. Cromek was travelling in that year in Dumfriesshire, partly with a view to a future Collection of Scottish songs, and he had the good fortune, as he deemed it, to make the acquaintance of Allan, then a youthful stone-mason of only twenty-five, earning eighteen shillings a week, and knowing much of the poetry of the district. When the idea occurred to Cromek of bringing out a volume of old songs collected from the peasantry, Allan undertook to collect what he could in Nithsdale and Galloway. In due course, when Cromek had returned to London, certain "ancient ballads" began to reach him from Cunningham: first the ballad " She's gane to dwall in Heaven," and then " Bonnie Lady Anne".

With the first ballad Cromek was justly delighted, declaring to its real author in a letter (27th October, 1809) that he did not know anything "more touching, more simply pathetic, in the whole range of Scottish song". But some acute criticism accompanied this eulogy. Could it be more than ninety years old? In old ballads there were no abstract ideas, like "gudeness," nor compound epithets, like "death-cold". As to the epithet "fell," that must have crept into the song through the ignorance of reciters ; it would have to be removed, and its removal not mentioned. But, despite these flaws, Cromek had read the verses to his old mother, his wife, sister and family, till all their hearts ached.

In the *Remains of Nithsdale and Galloway Song*, which Cromek published the year following (1810), with the collaboration of Cunningham, the ballad's age is referred to "about the time of the Reformation". Its subject was the daughter of the Laird Maxwell, of Cowhill, on the banks of the Nith, called by the peasantry "the lilie of Nithsdale," who died at nineteen. Cromek may have believed this, and expected the British public also to believe it.

But still more curious is the story in the same volume of the origin of " Bonnie Lady Anne ". It was alleged to have been introduced into Nithsdale about thirty years before by a lady of deranged mind, who wandered about, followed by some tamed sheep. She was mild and amiable, and would lie all night under some tree, with her sheep round her. These sheep were to her as daughters, eating of her bread, drinking of her cup. She used to sing this song unmoved till she came to the last verse, when she would burst into tears. The old tree, under which she generally sat, had been cut down, but whilst it stood the schoolboys paid it a sort of religious respect, and on fine Sabbath evenings the old women of the place would sit there, reading their Bibles, whilst the young men and maidens learned their Psalms, and "then went home full of the meek and holy composure of religion".

Truly Cunningham, whom Sir Walter Scott afterwards described as "honest Allan," had a most circumstantial imagination.   The *Remains*, of which Allan claimed the whole composition, "both poetry and prose," save two scraps, are probably as full of falsity as anything in the English language.   Among them is a poem "We were Sisters, we were Seven," of which he tells us that it was copied "from the recital of a peasant woman of Galloway, upwards of ninety years of age".   It was one of a "considerable number" copied from the same old woman, "all evidently productions of a very remote date," *i.e.*, the year 1810.   Well might Cunningham, writing to his brother on 10th September, 1810, make the following proud boast: "I could cheat a whole General Assembly of Antiquarians with my original manner of writing and forging ballads".   And from another letter (29th December, 1810) to the same brother, this is of interest about the *Remains*: "These songs and ballads being written for imposing on the country as the reliques of other years, I was obliged to have recourse to occasional coarseness, and severity, and negligence, which would make them appear as fair specimens of the ancient song and ballad".   O h! Honest Allan, so bashful when you first went to London that you really "could not utter a known

falsehood above three or four times a day," high is
the rank you won in the army of literary impostors.

Yet if Allan forged, he did it with great ability,
and the same path that led Chatterton to despair led
Cunningham to success. When the *Remains* appeared, they acquired an immediate reputation, though
most of the critics seem to have detected the fraud.
A single bound copy of the volume is said to have
been all that fell to Cunningham's share, who had
really composed almost the whole of it, ballads, introduction and notes, Cromek only being the editor or
publisher. Cromek himself died in March, 1812,
some fifteen months after the publication, and he is
supposed to have believed to the last in the genuineness of the ballads. But this is difficult to believe.
There is an undated letter from him to Cunningham,
in which he begs for the names of the Nithsdale and
Galloway poets; but he can hardly have been ignorant after, if not before, the publication, that the only
poet concerned was Cunningham himself. His
memory may be entitled to the benefit of the doubt,
but not even the excellence of the ballads forged as
ancient by Cunningham, nor the excellence and
success of much of his subsequent work, can free
Cunningham from the blame of a gross and cruel
deception practised on one who relied on his
honesty.

Even Motherwell, author of an excellent work
on *Minstrelsy: Ancient and Modern* (1827), did
not altogether escape from a temptation to which

Pinkerton, Surtees and Cunningham succumbed. The Cavalier's Song, beginning with—

A steed, a steed of matchless speede,
A sword of metal keene,

was introduced to the world as "written in an old hand in a copy of Lovelace's *Lucasta*, London, 1679," Motherwell himself being its real parent.

And if literary fraud of this kind was so easy and attractive in the eighteenth century, how much easier it must have been in earlier centuries, before experience had taught criticism the lesson of suspicion. What, for instance, should be thought of the verses, entitled "Majesty in Misery," said to have been composed by Charles I. during his captivity at Carisbrooke? Was he their real author? The evidence is far from satisfactory. Burnet, in his *Memoirs of James and William, Dukes of Hamilton* (1673), was the first to print them, and he did so on the authority of "a very worthy gentleman, who had the honour of waiting on him (the king) there, and was much trusted by him". This unnamed person it was who copied the verses from the original, and vouched for the truth of the copy (433). But if this gentleman had been as worthy as described, why should there have been this concealment of his name? One cannot but fear that he had no more material existence than those very old women on whom Surtees and Cunningham relied for the deception of the credulous.

If any one could have successfully "faked" a

ballad, it would have been Sir Walter Scott himself. His ballad of " Elspeth of the Burnfoot," in the battle of Harlaw, in the *Antiquary*, seems too good not to be antique. It can hardly be doubted that, both in " Kinmont Willie" and " Jamie Telfer," Scott wrote the four or five most stirring verses, helping out the weakness of the texts as they had reached him. Almost any reader can detect the hand of the master here and there. The business of the forger is to avoid being too poetical, and to shun a superfluity of old-fashioned words, while retaining a just measure of spirit in the narrative. If a man were allowed to lie freely about the source of his forgery, and to employ a scholarly writer of an old hand, using yellow old fly-leaves for paper, and ink rendered brown by well-known processes, he might even now deceive the experts.

CHAPTER XVI.

SOME MISCELLANEOUS FORGERIES.

It is inevitable in a survey of the large space occupied by forgery in literature that many instances of literary fraud should escape notice altogether. The view has to be comprehensive rather than exhaustive, and to confine itself to types and illustrations rather than to provide a mere catalogue of cases. The omission of several familiar flowers of artificial literature must find its excuse in this consideration ; the object being rather an impressionist picture than a canvas too crowded with detail.

There remain, however, still some cases of the craftsman's art, without some knowledge of which only an incomplete idea can be formed of the universality of the forger's genius. It will be seen that there is no province of the intellectual world which he has left uninvaded, no position so eminent as to have daunted him from the attempt to occupy it for himself. Both his skill and his audacity deserve, or even demand, some meed of a reluctant admiration.

In that portion of the literary field which is occupied by the thick crop of works of the imagination the forger has diligently sown his tares, and the names of some distinguished novelists have been borrowed by sundry literary adventurers. One would expect such names only to have been so borrowed when their models were no longer alive to expose the fraud ; but some have been so bold as to make free with an author's name even in his lifetime.

Of such was George W. Haering, who, under the pseudonym of Willibald Alexis, came to be one of Germany's first novelists in the early part of the nineteenth century. But he began with a work of bad promise, when in the year 1824 at the age of thirty-seven he published his first work, called *Walladmor.* At the Easter book-fairs at Leipsic it seems to have been common, in default of any new work of distinction, to publish some forgery as the work of some famous writer ; and to this custom *Walladmor* owed its birth. The book appeared as a free translation into German of a novel boldly ascribed to Sir Walter Scott ; and the next year it was as freely translated back again in London from German into English.

Prefixed to the third volume of this novel, Haering wrote a dedicatory preface to Sir Walter Scott, where-in he complained of his difficulty in having to trans-late the sheets just as they arrived dripping wet from the Edinburgh press, regardless either of sense or connexion. And he added : " The world pretends to doubt whether the novel is really yours. . . . From your obliging disposition, Sir Walter, I anticipate the

gratification of a few lines by the next post establishing the authenticity of *Walladmor*."

The German public, gulled by this impudent ruse,
greedily devoured the novel as indubitably Scott's;
and such was its success that three years later (1827)
the author made another attempt on the credulity of
his countrymen, by publishing another Scottian novel,
entitled *Scloss Avalon*.   In the preface to this Haering complained of the stupidity of people who had
failed to perceive in *Walladmor* a satirical attack
on the craze then prevalent for Scott's works; and
Julian Scmidt, in his *German Literature of the
Nineteenth Century* (iii., 261), to some extent accepts
this plea, contending that *Walladmor* only developed
into deliberate imitation after beginning with a merely
satirical intention.   But there was certainly no attempt
to make it clear to German readers that they were
being regaled with a satire on Scott, and not with
Scott himself: a distinction which is a fairly well-
marked one.   Haering was fortunate in finding a
public that was either forgetful or forgiving.

But most mimetic attempts on Scott hailed from
France.   Quérard ascribes to MM. Callet and
Pagnon two novels which were published at Paris
as being Scott's, each in two volumes: *Allan
Cameron* (1832) and *Aymé Verd* (1842).   In 1844
Charles J. David, son of the famous French painter,
introduced to the world as Scott's *La Pythie des
Highlands* in two volumes.   Born in 1783 David
was then sixty-one years of age, having been Pro-

fessor of Greek, first at Chios, then at Smyrna, and finally Professor of Greek Literature at Paris from 1831 to 1840. From so unlikely a source came this story of the Highland Pythoness, the half-crazy, half-inspired Mac-Maggy, who proves to be a Countess of Forfar, and who by her influence with the wild Highlanders induces them to rise in support of Prince Charles Edward in 1745. Both her character and that of Sir James Gregory, the Baillie of Ersnorth, are drawn with much cleverness after Scott's manner, and the whole atmosphere of the plot savours of Scott; but one can hardly believe that Scott could have described a disturbed grouse as rising "perpendicularly like an arrow" 300 feet into the air, and at that height being brought down by a gun (i., 209). Scott would never have accused a grouse of soaring into the sky like a lark.

The story of the novel was ingenious. The Abbé de la Rue, for fifty years a collector of old Norman ballads, had gone to England at the time of the French Revolution, and had there made the acquaintance of Scott, with whom he kept up a constant correspondence. When he died (about 1839), amongst a great bundle of papers was found this novel, with a dedicatory letter by Sir Walter, dated 1st December, 1831. Scott describes how, when the Abbé recited some of these old pieces, he listened with gaping mouth and strained ears; how writing down from memory these fragments on a sheet of paper he made them the epigraphs of chapters, which gradually swelled into a volume ; how he scrupled to print it when pressed to do so by Ballantyne, and therefore sent it to the Abbé, not intending to publish it till the Abbé's own projected work on Norman minstrelsy had first been published : which was not till 1834, two years after Scott's own death. It was from this book in three volumes on *Les Bardes Normands et Anglo-Normands* that David really drew all the epigraphs of his twenty chapters, at a date when it was no longer possible for Scott or the Abbé to disavow their mutual connexion.

In 1845 David published another novel as an unpublished one by Scott, called *Le Proscrit des Hebrides*, which describes how after the battle of Culloden the wonderful Mac-Maggy effected the escape of Charles Edward, on whose head alive or dead a reward of £30,000 had been placed, and how after marvellous adventures the object of her loyal devotion escaped in a vessel from the shores of Scotland. To this novel no preface was vouchsafed by its real author or by Scott.

More in the nature of a satire or parody than of a forgery was J. K. Paulding's *Lay of the Scottish Fiddle ; A Tale of Havre du Grace, Supposed to be written by Walter Scott, Esq.*, published in New York. But its editor claimed rather more for it than this in his preface. The poem had been sent to him by a friend in Edinburgh, where it was "universally attributed to Scott". A bookseller, after the brilliant naval feats of Admiral Cockburn in the Anglo-

American war in 1814, had asked Scott to celebrate them in a poem, and this he had done between a Monday and a Saturday. Nevertheless the editor would not vouch for its authenticity; though he adduced internal evidences of its genuineness.

But perhaps the most interesting of all the attempts to trade on Scott's name was that connected with the name of E. de Saint Maurice Cabany, Director-General of the Society of Archivistes of France, who in 1855 startled the literary world with a newly discovered novel by Scott, entitled *Moredun : A Tale of the* 1210. Messrs. Sampson Low, who published the work in England, vouched for their belief in the Frenchman's sincerity, and the very improbability of the story would of itself have seemed to entitle it to credence.

An eccentric German merchant in Paris (whose name even is not given), indebted to Cabany about the year 1825 for some literary assistance, left him at his death in 1831, when the decline of his fortunes admitted of no better gift, a simple writing-desk. But this desk never reached Cabany's possession till September, 1854; the merchant's widow and daughter having taken it away with them from Paris, and deeming the box of insufficient value to send to Cabany till the chance visit of a relative to Paris admitted of its conveyance thither free of charge. In this desk were some Royalist tracts; the MS. of *Moredun;* and a letter from W. S. (Walter Scott) to W. S. (William Spenser) dated 4th November,

1826 : which was the day after Spenser can be proved by Scott's *Journal* to have breakfasted with Scott at the Hotel Windsor in Paris.

The facsimile of this letter, prefixed to the published novel, shows a close resemblance to the writing of Scott, and though George Huntly Gordon, who had transcribed thirty-four volumes of Scott's novels in the days of his anonymity, found fault with some of the letters, there is no doubt that, if not by Sir Walter's hand, both the letter of 4th November and all the three volumes of the novel were composed in the most exact imitation of his handwriting.

According to this letter, Sir Walter, who had previously made a gift of *Moredun* to his daughter Anne, persuaded her to transfer it to his friend Spenser (the author of *The Grave of Gelert* and other poems) for the sake of the German merchant, whilst himself believing that the said merchant was none other than Spenser himself.   In making the gift Sir Walter only stipulated that, if Spenser ever published it, he should publish it under his own initials, and should do all he fairly could to publish it as really "a bairn of his ain".

Such was Cabany's story of his acquisition of the novel : Scott gave it to Spenser ; who gave or sold it to the German ; who left it to Cabany.   And the German had often spoken of his possession or expected possession of a manuscript by Scott, of whom, as of Goethe, he was an ardent admirer.

18

Improbable as this story is, it contains at first sight no flagrant impossibility. And the novel itself has something of Scott's style as well as of his handwriting : an interview between King John of England and William the Lion of Scotland vividly recalls the interview in *Quentin Durward* between Louis XI. of France and Charles, Duke of Burgundy. But there is one little point which alone seems absolutely fatal to Cabany's story. There occurs the following allusion to Newcastle : "In one of the narrow streets which wound up tortuously from the Sandhill to the Castle of Newcastle-upon-Tyne, some traces of which still resist the improving hands of time, money, and Granger". This passage must have been written after Granger had laid his improving hand on the town. But it was not before 1832, the year of Scott's death, that Granger bought for £50,000 those sites in Newcastle which he afterwards so much embellished ; nor was it before a Thursday in May, *1834*, that a meeting of the Common Council held a meeting to consider his plans (Richardson's *Guide to Newcastle*, 325). How then could Scott in a novel given to Spenser in 1826 have had this prophetic knowledge of Granger's improvements?

This Granger allusion is surely an insuperable obstacle to a belief in Scott's authorship. But what then becomes of Cabany's story of the old man often alluding to such a possession as actual or prospective, or of his having left it in a writing-desk? For he

is said to have died in 1831, and no one can have
written that passage about Granger during Scott's
lifetime.   No one therefore can have palmed off
such a work on the old German, and it is difficult to
see how Cabany's story of his connexion with the
novel can be otherwise than deliberately false.

Nor can any one have palmed it off upon Cabany ;
for how should any one have known about the
German and the writing-desk ?   The whole responsibility seems thus to be thrown upon Cabany : between whom and Scott the choice of parentage lies.
Yet Cabany's honesty was unsuspected by his
English publishers, and a more plausible story would
surely have lain open to his invention.   The mystery
must remain unsolved.   Whoever the culprit was,
he had a most intimate knowledge of English topography ; he knew well the country about Hexham ;
had seen the remarkable thirteenth century monument to a lady and child in Scarcliffe Church ; and
described, in a chapter headed "Ingleborough," the
Craven district of Yorkshire, the Ebbing and Flowing
well at Giggleswick, and the Weathercote Cave near
Ingleton, with a fidelity that could hardly have come
save from actual knowledge of the district.   It is
possible, though hardly probable, that a Frenchman
might have had such knowledge.

Next to Scott the name of Mrs. Ann Radcliffe,
best known by her *Mysteries of Udolpho*, has been
of most frequent service to writers whose diffidence
of their own powers to attract has tempted them to

18 *

trade on the powers of others. Mrs. Radcliffe's re-
liance for effect on ruined castles and spectres opened
up a field of temptingly easy cultivation, and she
accordingly found herself compelled to disown in the
English press numerous different romances with
which her name became falsely connected. That
very prolific French writer, the Baron de Lamothe-
Langon, who seems to have regarded all literary
names as common property, published two novels as
translations from Mrs. Radcliffe, of which he was himself the sole author : one was *L'Hermite de la tombe
Mysterieuse*, which professed to be by Mrs. Radcliffe
extracted from some annals of the thirteenth century,
and to have been translated by De Langon (1815); the
other was the *Mystères de la Tour St. Jean*, also purporting to be a translation from Mrs. Radcliffe (1818).

But the most interesting of these Radcliffe works
is the *Rose d'Altenberg, ou le Spectre dans les ruines*,
translated in 1830 by M. Henri Duval from an
English manuscript said to have been found "in the
portfolio of the late Ann Radcliffe". This book enjoyed an eventful career under several aliases. First
of all it appeared in 1813 as *Alexina*, a four-volumed
novel imitated from the English by Mme. Brayer
de Saint-Leon ; then Mrs. Campbell published a
translation of it as her own work in 1821 as *The
Midnight Wanderer;* and finally M. Duval brought
back the *Wanderer* to France by re-translating it as
the *Rose d'Altenberg*, recovered from the capacious
Radcliffe portfolio.

The Memoirs, Letters, or Souvenirs of distinguished people occupy the borderland between pure fiction and history, and offer naturally a rich harvest to the historian. But they are thickly strewn with traps for the unwary, and call for the exercise of much circumspection. Unwise indeed would he be who should attempt to draw truth from these deep wells of deception unaided by Quérard's monumental dictionary of literary deception. (*Supercheries Littéraires Dévoilées*).

Take, for instance, Frederic II. of Prussia; for him alone were invented by different writers his *Pensées sur la Religion*; his *Dernières Pensées*; his *Bréviaire Philosophique*; his *Matinées du Roi du Prusse*; his *Conseils du Trône* to the kings and peoples of Europe; to say nothing of some unpublished letters, and a Testament.

No topic was a greater favourite with inventive writers than such political testaments. Besides Frederic, Cardinals Richelieu and Alberoni, Rousseau, Voltaire, Colbert, and the Emperor Joseph II., all left the world the richer for legacies of wisdom for which they are not responsible.

It is only possible to skim the surface of this bottomless sea. To Lamothe-Langon, the translator of two of the imaginary novels by Mrs. Radcliffe, we owe in addition four volumes of *Memoirs* by Mme. du Barry; six volumes of *Memoirs* by Richelieu (1829); and four volumes of *Memoirs* by Talleyrand (1838). And for all who go to history for amusement rather than for truth these ingenious fabrications are not lacking in charm. They often give the aroma of a period better than works that profess a greater regard for actuality. Of such are the interesting *Souvenirs* of the Marquise de Créquy, from 1710 to 1803, supposed to be addressed to her grandson, but mainly composed, possibly with some aid from the Marquise, by M. Cousin, Comte de Courchamps, who first published them in seven volumes at Paris in 1834 ; and lately (1904) reproduced in England in abridged form under the title of *The French Noblesse of the Eighteenth Century* by Mrs. Colquhoun Grant. A work of similar style and merit is ascribed to the Marquis Barbé-Marbois, who published in London in 1774 four small volumes of letters for which Mme. de Pompadour was claimed as the author between 1753 and 1762. It was a clever compilation, to which the use of contemporary anecdotes lent a misleading semblance of truth. The editor's story was that he had bought the letters from the executor of that famous lady's secretary, who had then lately died in Holland. But of such stories and of such works the name is Legion.

A conclusion of forgeries in these miscellaneous paths of literature may fitly be made with one which gave no small occupation to criticism in the early days of the nineteenth century. When Charles Vanderbourg published in 1803 the first edition of the poems of Marguerite - Eleonore - Clotilde de

Vallon - Chalys, afterwards Mme. de Surville, the book had a great success. Of this Clotilde Vanderbourg told the following amazing story : that in the fifteenth century she produced works which surpassed in style and versification anything previously connected with so early a date. Born in 1405, she wrote wonderful verses at the age of ten or twelve, and subsequently became the centre of a school of French poetesses, of whose names the world then heard for the first time. Married in 1421 to Berenger de Surville, she composed, on his early forsaking his bride for the battle-field, a remarkable poem, called *L'Heroide*, whose merits so excited the jealousy of the poet Alain Chartier that Clotilde never again sought publicity for her later inspirations. After surviving her husband, her son, her daughter and her granddaughter, she closed her poetical career in her ninety-fourth year by a poem addressed to Charles VIII. in celebration of his victory at the battle of Fornoue in 1495.

Vanderbourg professed to have derived both the poems and the story of Clotilde from Joseph Etienne de Surville, a descendant of the poetess, born in 1755. This Joseph led a soldier's life ; emigrated from France at the Revolution ; and on his return to France was shot in 1798. Joseph's story was that he had found his ancestress' poems whilst rummaging among some old family archives ; but of the manuscript so discovered there is no evidence of any eye-witness but himself. He also found several books of *Memoirs* written by his ancestress, and it was from these *Memoirs*, never published by himself, that Vanderbourg drew for his sketch of a line of French mediæval poetesses previously unknown to fame.

So wonderful a story naturally gave rise to the questions : Were these poems genuine? Had Clotilde ever been clothed in flesh and blood? And had Joseph de Surville really found these poems and *Memoirs*, or had he invented both them and his ancestress together? Errors and anachronisms came to be discovered, and a modern spirit to be detected beneath the mediæval language. Vanderbourg (1765-1827) fell himself under much suspicion, from which his memory was not fully rescued till 1863 by three articles which Macé wrote in the *Journal de l'Instruction Publique* (31st January, 4th February, and 28th March, 1863). Vanderbourg had argued that Joseph was quite incapable of writing poems of such excellence as those ascribed to Clotilde ; but the fraud, which the criticisms of Villemain and Sainte-Beuve ultimately laid bare, can be laid to the charge of no one else. One is left to wonder that a poet capable of producing poems so good as Clotilde's were admitted to be should have spent some years of his life in building up a reputation for an imaginary ancestress when he might with no more labour have permanently established his own. But to many minds the mere deception of the world carries its own exceeding great reward.

Another collection of Clotilde's poems (*Poesies inédites*) saw the light at Paris in 1826, but this collection was chiefly remarkable for the reckless boldness of some of its anachronisms. Clotilde therein defended the Copernican system at a time when Copernicus must have been a mere boy ; she refuted Lucretius at a time when there were no printed copies of Lucretius to refute ; and she alluded to the satellites of the planet Saturn, though the first of them was not discovered till 140 years after her death. But criticism has reason to be thankful when the facilities or temptations of literary mimicry perplex it with a problem no harder than this.

.   .   .   .

And with this poor fraud ends our cursory survey of the more eminent figures in the world's well-filled gallery of forgers. It is a mixed as well as a crowded gallery, where some are known, and some are nameless, and where not all are deserving of the same degree of condemnation. Audacious, designing, but interesting figures, who, in revolt against the world's conventional standard, employed letters, as other men freely and without censure employ politics : some for mere pecuniary ends, some for the slaking of political passion, some for the sheer joy of deceiving their fellows, or of exercising and displaying their abilities. The conscience of mankind esteems literary purity as of higher sanctity than purity in political conduct, and thus the world turns a condemning frown on the literary adventurer,

whilst reserving its condoning smile for his politica
counterpart.   But if we accept the world's verdic
in this respect as roughly just, let us remember tha
it was their exceptional talents which were generally
these sinners' temptations, and that a merciful nature
by denying to most of us an equality of gifts, has
preserved us from a similar struggle with the moral
law.   A blurred vision was theirs, disabling them
from discerning clearly between truth and falsity,
between fact and fiction ; but let it at least be
accounted some atonement for this moral defect
that their endeavours reached often no mean level of
intellectual excellence, and that their worst trickeries
paid a kind of inverted tribute to the honour and
glory of literature.

DATE DUE
